Old Salem at Sea

~ in ballad and song ~

Old Salem at Sea

~ in ballad and song ~

Part II of the series

Old Salem ~ in ballad and song ~ Part I of the series

Researched and Compiled by

ROBERT E. STROM

Foreword by Daisy Nell

CABOT FARM, PUBLISHER SALEM, MASSACHUSETTS

Copyright © 2020 by Robert E. Strom

Researched and Compiled by Robert E. Strom

Foreword by Daisy Nell

All rights reserved. No part of this book may be reproduced in any form or by electronic or mechanical means without written permission from the publisher except by a reviewer who may quote brief passages in a review.

Library of Congress Cataloging and publication data has been applied for.

ISBN: 978-0-578-71282-6

Printed in the United States

Published by Cabot Farm Publisher,
Salem, Massachusetts

Website: Bobandjenstrom.com
email: Bobstrom10@comcast.net

Foreword

What is it about songs of the sea that touch the spark of romance, with wistful recollections of our lives at sea, near the sea, or just on our life's journey? It is said that the sea is what separates the people of the world, and is also what connects us.

Salem, Massachusetts, is synonymous with the maritime history of America. Her early ventures in the China Trade and the shoreside support industries kept Salem in the forefront from the late 18th century, just after the Revolution, to the middle of the 19th Century. Bob Strom has assembled these songs, ballads, and shanties in *Old Salem at Sea in Ballad and Song*. The accounts of voyages, through logbooks, journals, and print media have recorded the role of music before, during and about these voyages. Strom presents this collection by topic, such as Superstition, Prison Logbooks, Life and Death at Sea, and Bold Sea Captains. This collection represents extensive research of songs with universal themes, such as a treacherous captain, a faithful lass, the stormy seas, and the rich rewards of patriotism, heroism, and survival.

A familiar theme of the sailor is longing for home when far away at sea, and the yearning for the shipboard life once more, when "Jack" is home at last.

From the *Salem Gazette*, 1808, the song *Yankee Jack*:

> Jack cast a tearful eye around
> And thought upon his native valley
> And mid the pealing thunder's sound
> His voice was heard, 'Farewell, my Sally'

From *A Sailor's Life*, in the *Salem Gazette*, c 1810:

> Then under full sail we laugh at the gale
> Though the landsmen look pale, never heed 'em
> But toss off the glass to a favourite lass
> To America, Commerce, and Freedom

    Some of these ballads bore tales with almost fairytale-like endings, endlessly entertaining to sailors in their long hours at sea. In their off-watch hours songs and ballads were often sung, whether accompanied by fiddle or other portable instruments brought from home. One such song is *Billy Taylor*, where the sailor lad who is pressed into sea service is pursued by his lover. She dresses in boy's clothing and passes as a deckhand, only to be discovered by the captain after she proves her prowess. He tells her that young Billy Taylor had gotten married to another girl. Upon hearing this, the young maid shoots poor old Billy, and the captain rewards her with a promotion to lieutenant and the command of a ship.

    Fair Salem Town tells a familiar tale of the "broken token", with the story of a returning sailor who disguises himself to test his true love's faithfulness. When she demonstrates her loyalty by answering all of his questions correctly, he matches his half of a ring, or "token", to her half and they live happily ever after. What sailor could resist believing that his luck would be the same when he returns?

    Worth noting for clarity, one can find sailors' work songs, or shanties, spelled in various sources as "chanteys", or even "chants". Often thought to have originated from the French verb chanter, meaning to sing, these rhythmic ditties created a relief from the tedium of hard hauling or pulling of lines, manning the pumps, and adjusting the sails required to keep the ship working. Salem ships were often away for a year or longer, traveling beyond Cape Horn or the Cape of Good Hope, through uncharted and pirated waters. Many vessels had their own favorite songs for specific tasks or times, such as raising the anchor or setting the sails for the outward or homeward bound passages. The life aboard each ship fostered its own culture of songs for work and pleasure, creating a loyalty, camaraderie, and even courage that served them well during their voyages.

Some songs were written to honor Salem's heroes such as Elias Haskett Derby and Nathaniel Bowditch, and some to honor the actual vessels, such as the *Friendship* and *Fame*, both of which are kept alive in spirit today by their recently built replicas in Salem Harbor, over 100 years later. Like these vessels, the songs and shanties are still viable today, cherished and sung, as many local musicians, including author Bob Strom and his wife Jennifer Strom, who carry on this timeless and infectious repertoire.

> I wonder what's the dreadful row
> They're kicking up in Portsmouth now
> The people running up and down
> Crying 'All Salem's come to town!'
> -From *Witch of the Wave*

~ Daisy Nell

[Singer, songwriter, schooner skipper, former manager of School Programs at the Peabody Essex Museum, Chair of the annual Gloucester Schooner festival, author of 6 children's books, including *The Stowaway Mouse*, 2012 Penrose Press]

Contents

Foreword v

Introduction xv

I. OFF TO CALIFORNIA
I Came From Salem City
    Music *Oh Susanna* by Stephen Foster 2
The California Gold Diggers by Jesse Hutchison, Jr.
    Music by Dan Emmett 5
I've Been Dreamin' by Bill Adams 10
Witch of the Wave 12
Witch of the Wave, fiddle tune 16
Gold 17
The Gold Hunter's Story by Chat Hunt 18
The Returned Californian by James Pierpont
    & arranged by John P. Ordway 20

II. SUPERSTITION
The Mermaid 24
Of the Lost Ship
    by Eugene Richard White 27
The Gosport Tragedy or The Ship's Carpenter 29

III. SALEM SHIP and PRISON LOG BOOKS
Hills of Georgetown 34
Lines composed on a court martial of Oliver Poland
    for the theft on board The America 35
The Sailor's Early Home
    by Rev. S. D. Phelps 37

Of Dartmore Prison
    by Joseph Valpey, Jr. 39
Hunting for Lice and Fleas
    by Joseph Valpey, Jr. 41
The Fruits of Gambling's
    by Joseph Valpey, Jr. 42
Ship Bengal at Sea 44
The Greenland Whale 46
The Sea Ran High or On the Loss
    of Schooner Mechanic Captain Holland 49
The Captain calls All Hands 50
Sharply Its Breath the Vessel Feels 51
Blow! Oh Blow! 52
Merrily, Merrily! 52
The Wandering Sailor 53
The Faithful Sailor 54

IV. LIFE AT SEA

Home Again
    by Marshall S. Pike 58
The Seaman 60
The Sailor's Watch At Sea 61
A Sailor's Life 62
The Sailor Boy 63
A Sea Song 65
Heaving the Anchor 66
The Fisherman's Orphan 68
Written at Sea in a Heavy Gale 70
The Honest Sailor
    by Charles Dibdin 72
Harriet Low
    by Daisy Nell 74

Again to Mary Dear 76
The Seaman's Home 77
Come All Good People
    by Edward Beacham 78
Fair Salem Town (A Seaman and His Love) 80
Sweet William and Gentle Jenny 82
The Disconsolate Sailor
    by Joseph Valpey, Jr. 84
Living in a Seaport Town by Gerry Ryan 86

V. DEATH AT SEA
On The Death of A Tar 90
The Dying Sailor Boy 92
Bury Me, Bury Me, Quick, Quick
    by Phineas Stowe 94
Bury Me, Bury Me, Quick, Quick part II
    by Phineas Stowe 96
Burn the Ships by Phineas Stowe 97
Melancholy Situation by Jonathan Plummer 100
Yankee Jack 102
Blow on! Blow on! The Pirate's Glee
   or Storm at Sea in a Schooner
    by Arthur Morrill 103
The Tale of the Sea
    by F. E. Weatherly 104
Dame Alice Was Sitting on Widow's Walk 106
The Mariner's Grave 110

VI. COMMERCE
A Ship Comes In Salem 1830
    by Oliver Jenkins 114
Derby Street - Salem: Present Day
    by Oliver Jenkins 115

Unknown Title
    by the son of Rev Charles Timothy Brooks 117
Launching of the "Grand Turk" 118
Th' Embargo 120
Baker's Island Light 122
Oh Grant That Pleasant Be 123
Ye Golden Lamps of Heaven! Farewell
    by Philip Doddridge 124

VII. BOLD SEA CAPTAINS

The Fame of Salem 128
Bold Hathorne or
    "The Cruise of the Fair American" 130
Manly 133
Billy Taylor 136
Occasioned by the arrival of the remains of
    Lawrence and Ludlow at Salem 140
The Battle of Quallah Battoo 146
Peace Party 150
The Loss off (of) Sir John Franklin 152

VIII. CAPTAIN EDWARD B. TRUMBULL

Captain Trumbull 157
Tom Pepper 160
Kizee Makazee - Yah 164
Zanzibar Work Song 165
Sally Brown 165
Blow The Man Down 166
Santa Anna 168
Old Horse 168
One More Day 169
Bound for the Rio Grande 170
Ruben Ranzo 172

Table of Content

The Wide Missouri 174
The Dreadnaught 176
Blow, Boys Blow!. 178
Hoodah Day 180
Whisky Johnny 182
My Own Country 184
Haul The Bowline 186

Acknowledgments 189
Endnotes 191
Bibliography 209
Web Resources 215
Blog 216
Shipping and Prison Log Journals 217
Chapter Tune References 218
Photographs, Postcards,
    Clippings, Maps 219
Index 223

Introduction

Old Salem at Sea in Ballad and Song is a collection of sea songs and ballads that reflects Salem's rich maritime history and its relationship to the sea. The ballads in this book tell stories of whaling ships and the dangers they encountered. The sea songs narrate the trials of Salem privateers, and tell of adventures to far-off lands, loneliness, missed loved ones, and of home. The sea shanties were sung by sailors to lighten the workload, while some songs were sung on board for entertainment, and to pass the time.

Over the last several years, I have culled through numerous sources to collect the material for *Old Salem In Ballad and Song*. In this second book, *Old Salem at Sea in Ballad and Song*, I have presented 89 songs and ballads that all have a connection to Salem and the sea. Some of the pieces in this book have been written in shipping logbooks, published on broadsides, in songbooks, or in periodicals, and while many will be familiar, several of the songs or variants may be new or different to the reader. Most the material in this book comes from public domain sources. On occasion, I have altered one or two words from a ballad for clarity and understanding. The term shanties come from the French word chantez, to sing, and through this book you will notice several different spellings of the word: shanty, chantey, or chanty. Each spelling was taken from the history or the background (i.e., bark or barque) of that particular song. While some of the songs have tunes associated with them, and many can be sung to airs or tunes familiar to the singer, others do not, giving the singer freedom to make up their own tune.

Trade from Salem's relatively small harbor began to shrink in the early to mid-1800s, taken by much larger ports on the east coast. With the discovery of gold in California, Salem sea captains began building and sailing fast clipper ships, and transporting gold hunters and supplies to San Francisco. As ships left Salem harbor, songs were sung and recorded in the ships' log journals. Some of these new songs were newly written, and sung to popular tunes of the time.

Stephen Foster tunes were used in songs like the *Banks of the Sacramento (Camptown Races)* and *I Come From Salem City (Oh! Suzanna)* as the ships left Salem while several of his songs like *Gentle Annie* and *Old Folks at Home* were written in log journals for remembrance, entertainment or to just pass the time. *I Come from Salem City,* using the tune of *Oh! Susanna* was recorded and sung aboard the *Bark Eliza* as it left Derby Wharf in Salem on December 23, 1848. During that same time period, Isaac Baker had written the company song, *The San Francisco Company,* out of Beverly, Massachusetts, also sung to the tune of *Oh! Susanna,* as a "Thanksgiving proclamation for the company and crew." [1] The ship's log keeper, Joseph Carrico wrote the song in the Journal of the voyage *Barque San Francisco 1849 - 1850.* [1]

We started from Old Beverly,
Mid cheers from great and small,
We hope to get back bye and bye
When we'll return them all.

The day we left the wind was fair,
And pleasant was the sky,
The fair sex wept, the boys hurrahed
And we'd no time to cry.

Chorus: O! California,
We'll see you bye and bye
If we've good luck, and if we don't,
Why, bless you, don't you cry.

Introduction

While combing through shipping logbooks at the Phillips Library, it was fascinating to see the original journals and documents Gale Huntington found and wrote about. Gale Huntington is from Martha's Vineyard and for a short time, lived in Nahant, Massachusetts. Huntington was born in 1902 and died in 1993. He is best known for his work; *Songs the Whalemen Sang* first published in 1964. Huntington spent hours at museums throughout New England combing through logbooks of whaling ships, clipper ships, and merchant ships looking for sea shanties, ballads, songs, and poems related to life aboard a seafaring vessel. Huntington also spent some time at the Peabody Museum and the Essex Institute in Salem, Massachusetts, researching important Salem shipping logbooks like those of the *Bengal, Lotos, Ann, La Grange, Vaughan,* and *Richmond.*

Huntington transcribed and researched each song from the logbooks and discovered never-before-published songs, and various versions of ballads, sea songs, and sea shanties some being local to Salem, New England, and the seafaring community throughout the world.

The song *Hearts of Gold,* found in the 1832 journal of the whale ship *The Bengal* out of Salem, Massachusetts, was originally found by Gale Huntington and published in *Songs the Whalesmen Sang* and also recorded by Stuart Frank on his LP *Songs of the Sea and Shore.* Huntington states: "This has no title in the *Bengal* journal so I have called it *Hearts of Gold* which seems to be the important phrase." [2] The first two verses being:

> It was the plowing of the raging seas
> Was always my delight?
> While those loving old landlubbers
> No dangers do they know?

> Not like we long Jack Hearts of Gold
> Who plow the ocean through?
> Not like we long Jack Hearts of Gold
> Who plow the ocean through?

Huntington also co-authored with Lani Herrmann *Sam Henry's Songs of the People*, published by University of Georgia Press in 2010. *Songs of the People* is considered a comprehensive collection of Irish songs, ballads, and fiddle tunes. *The Gam, More Songs the Whalemen Sang* [3] is the sequel to *Songs the Whalemen Sang* that was released after his death in 2014. [4] In 1993, Larry Kaplan wrote a song for Gale Huntington called *Song for Gale* on his CD named *Worth All the Telling*, [5] a Folk-Legacy recording.

Another ballad of interest that Huntington found was *Bonaparte*, from the 1834 journal of the *L. C. Richmond* of Salem and found in the Essex Institute Collection in Salem, Massachusetts. He published the song in *Songs the Whalemen Sang*. Listed in the journal, Huntington reports that the manuscript copy calls the song *Bonny Parte*. [6]

> Come all you natives far and near
> Come listen to my song and story
> Of these few lines you soon shall hear
> How soon a man is deprived of glory.
>
> Ambition it will have its fling
> Fortune backwards it will twiddle
> Boni would not be content
> Until he was master of the whole world.
> Fal de ral etc.

There has always been a bounty of songs about Bonaparte over the years. John Bertram, a famous sea captain from Salem, sailed by St. Helena and wanted to visit Bonaparte but was not allowed on the island. Bertram wrote a letter to Bonaparte that went unanswered.

Frederick Pease Harlow wrote *The Making of a Sailor* [7] and also transcribed sea shanties, not from shipping logbooks like Huntington, but from sailors aboard the ship *Akbar*. Harlow's *The Making of a Sailor* is considered by many to be one of the best sea narratives written and was published by the Marine Research Society of Salem, Massachusetts in 1928. *Chanteying Aboard American Ships* [8] was posthumously published in 1962 at the insistence and under the guidance of Ernest Dodge of the Peabody Museum of Salem. [9]

Harlow states in *Chanteying Aboard American Ships*, that he remembered "shanties sung aboard the ship Akbar on a trip from Massachusetts to Melbourne, Australia in 1876. A crewmate "Dave" is said to have taught this (song) to the crew while pumping at the windlass." [10] *South Australia* or *Rollin' King*, a popular shanty still sung today, can be sung using floating verses or a combination of the general shanty repertoire and improvised verses depending on the moment or the individual singer. [11, 12] The first verse of *South Australia* or *Rollin' King* is:

> South Australia is my native land,
> Heave a-way! Heave a-way!
> Mountains rich with quarts and sand.
> I'm bound for South Australia.
>
> Heave a-way! Heave a-way!
> Heave a-way, you Ruler king,
> I'm bound for South Australia.

Harlow's version of *South Australia/ Rollin' King*, uses the common term for a prostitute, "Julia," to describe the sailors' feelings of comfort and familiarity upon finding a woman. Julia's name could be changed depending on the port the seamen were in or their new acquaintance.

"Julia sling the she-oak at the bar
And welcomes sailors from afar."

South Australia/ Rollin' King also has references to Sheoak. "Sheoak is the name of high proof, keg beer made in southern Australia" [12] Harlow also mentioned that the sailors can sing South Australia while hoisting the anchor around the capstan.

Another example of a song sung to a popular melody of the time is Harlow's version of *Dixie's Isle*, sung to the tune of *Oh! Susanna*. With the chorus being:

Oh then Susie, lovely Susie,
I can no longer stay,
For the bugle sounds the warning
That calls me far away. [12]

Stan Hugill in his book, *Shanties From the Seven Seas* [13] listed several versions of Harlow's shanties including:

The Girl in Portland Street
or *Whistling Shanty or Fal-de-lal-day*
Drunken Sailor / Hooray Up She Rises

Sea captain and politician Nathanial Silsbee of Salem contributed several sea songs and shanties to the repertoire. William Main Doerflinger states in his book *Songs of the Sailor and Lumberman* that Silsbee "preserved in manuscript form about seventy shanties and other sailorman's songs as he learned them at sea." [14] While researching, songs have been unearthed by log keeper George Silsbee, Nathanial Silsbee in the late 1700s and early 1800s, and

Introduction

Nathanial Silsbee Jr. but the bulk of the shanties that Silsbee's niece Mrs. George C. Beach of New York kept that were dated 1893 are still missing. Maybe some day the balance of Silsbee's versions will surface.

Doerflinger was first to publish the now well-known song *Come Down You Bunch of Red Roses* (attributed to Silsbee). Below are the first two verses of the song.

> Oh, yes, my lads, we'll roll alee,
> > Go down, you blood red roses, go down!
> We'll soon be far away from sea,
> > Go down, you blood red roses, go down!
>
> Oh, you pinks and posies,
> > Go down, you blood red roses, go down!
>
> Oh, yes, my lads, we'll roll alee,
> > Go down, you blood red roses, go down!
> We'll soon be far away from sea,
> > Go down, you blood red roses, go down!
>
> Oh, you pinks and posies,
> > Go down, you blood red roses, go down!

Harlow in his book *The Making of a Sailor* gives another version of the *Bunch of Roses Shanty* with a different tune. He writes that he heard it sung by the shanty man aboard his ship. Handsome Charlie would begin singing when sweating-up halyards or swigging (swaying). [15]

> Oh Mary! Come down, with your bunch of roses,
> Come down when I call, Oh Mary!
> Oh Mary, come down!

Another song attributed to Nathaniel Silsbee found in Doerflinger's book *Songs of the Sailor and Lumberman* is *John Dameray*. [14]

A loft we all must go-oh,
    John come down the backstay
In hail and frost and snow-oh,
    John come down the backstay, John Dameray!

    John Dameray - John come down the backstay
    John Dameray - John come down the backstay
        John Demeray!
    John Dameray - John come down the backstay
    John Dameray - John come down the backstay
        John Demeray!

My Ma she wrote to me,
    John come down the backstay
"My son, come home from seas"
    John come down the backstay, John Dameray!

Got no manay and no clothes
    John come down the backstay
Am knocking out of doors.
    John come down the backstay, John Dameray!

My home I soon will be in,
    John come down the backstay
And then we'll have some gin.
    John come down the backstay, John Dameray!

From sea I will keep clear,
    John come down the backstay
And live by selling beer.
    John come down the backstay, John Dameray!

Introduction

Finally, Captain Edward B. Trumbull of 90 Federal Street Salem, Massachusetts was one of the last sea captains to sail out of Salem. Trumbull was Captain of the *Taria Topan* and president of the Marine Society of Salem from 1916-1934, treasurer from 1904-1934 and clerk from 1894-1904. Trumbull contributed 18 song variations to James Carpenter's collection of ballads, songs and sea shanties put together as part of Carpenter's PhD dissertation called *Forecastle Songs and Chanties* while attending Harvard University. All of Trumbull's versions that were given to Carpenter are included in this book.

Singers and balladeers from time past have given us the songs for *Old Salem at Sea in Ballad and Song*. Salem's rich and fascinating maritime history is reflected through its music and how it fits into the broader New England and our country, and the maritime communities throughout the world. Whether sailors left Salem and headed to California on clipper ship or on whaling expeditions, songs were sung. Popular songs of the day were sung for entertainment around the forecastle or sea shanties could be sung to lighten the workload. Several of these songs were written in log journals, which also documented weather conditions, punishments and distances traveled. The song tradition continues to live on today with contemporary songs written in the folk tradition about Salem's maritime past. The *Fame of Salem* is an example of a contemporary song written by Larry Young in 2003 and sung by *Ye Mariners All*. I hope you get to know these ballads and sing these songs. The folk music community of today is keeping the tradition alive with ongoing shanty sings and pub sings throughout New England and the world.

~ Bob Strom

A Noble Company [16]

A noble company, that early band,
Who left their homes to sail across the sea;
And distance voyages to the orient planned,
The land of wealth and dark Idolatry.

Behold their monuments! The rich and rare,
Gathered, with cost and pains, from every clime?
So interest and instinct the future time;
To cherish in their sons, the spirit brave,

Which gave to Salem its world-wide renown,
That thus their exploits, on the ocean wave,
From age to age might still be handed down,
And guard their trust, more precious then? Their gold.

SILSBEE FAMILY PAPERS

~ 1 ~
Off to California

(Oh! Suzanna)

I Come From Salem City

The song *I Come From Salem City* or *Oh! California* as it is sometimes called was first sung on the *Bark Eliza* to the tune of *Oh! Susanna* by Stephen Foster. [1] *Oh! Susanna* was published in 1847 and launched Foster's career as a songwriter. [2] Foster's songs soon became a favorite with minstrel troupes and associated with the California Gold Rush of 1849. According to Alfred Peabody in his article *On The Early Days and Rapid Growth of California* printed in the Essex Institute Collection, "this song was composed for the occasion of sailing from Derby Wharf on December 23, 1848 to California. It was called the *California Song* and sung on board of every vessel going around Cape Horn and by immigrants over the plains." [3]

The *Bark Eliza's* owner, John Bertram of Salem, was one of the first ship owners to take advantage of the possibilities of trade around Cape Horn to San Francisco. [4] Bertram realized that there was a "scarcity and high price of provisions," including mining implements, houses and lumber. [3] The voyage from Salem lasted 160 days, the bark arriving in California on June 1, 1849. With this success, Bertram went on to build famous clipper ships for the California trade in deeper harbors, the *John Bertram* in East Boston and the *Witch of the Wave* in Portsmouth, New Hampshire. [4]

According to Frank Shay, the version of the song *I Come From Salem City* found in his book, *American Sailor's Treasury: Sea Chanteys, Legends and Lore*, has had a long and happy life, unlike most parodies of this song. [5]

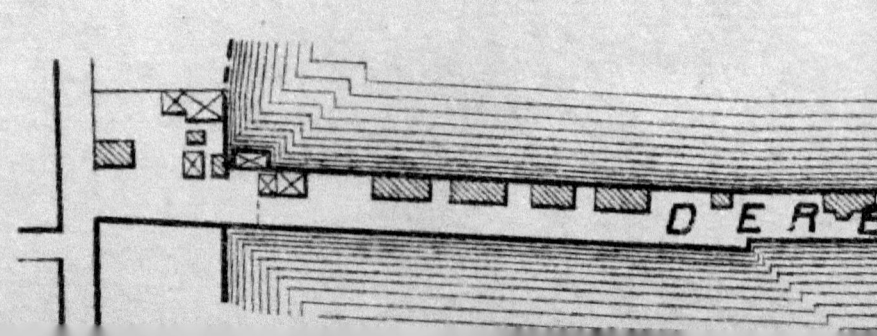

Off To California

I come from Salem City,
With my washbowl on my knee.
I'm going to California
The gold dust for to see.
It rained all night the day I left,
The weather it was dry,
The sun so hot I froze to death
Oh, brothers, don't you cry!

    Chorus: Oh, California,
               That's the land for me!
               I'm bound for San Francisco
               With my washbowl on my knee!

I jumped aboard the 'Liza ship
And traveled on the sea,
And every time I thought of home
I wished it wasn't me!
The vessel reared like any horse
That had of oats a wealth;
I found it wouldn't throw me, so
I thought I'd throw myself!

    Chorus: Oh, California,
               That's the land for me!
               I'm bound for San Francisco
               With my washbowl on my knee!

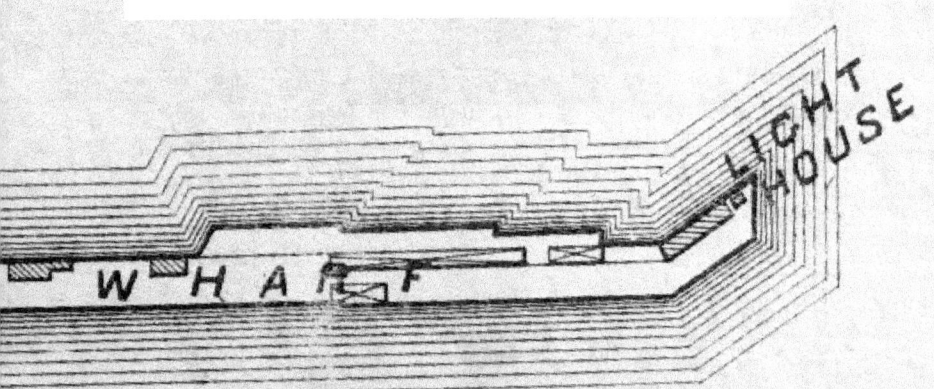

I thought of all the pleasant time
We've had together here,
I thought I ought to cry a bit,
But couldn't find a tear.
The pilot bread was in my mouth,
The gold dust in my eye,
And though I'm going far away,
Dear brothers, don't you cry!

      Chorus: Oh, California,
                   That's the land for me!
                   I'm bound for San Francisco
                   With my washbowl on my knee!

I soon shall be in 'Frisco,
And there I shall look around,
And when I see the gold lumps there
I'll pick them off the ground.
I'll scrape the mountains clean, my boys,
I'll drain the rivers dry,
A pocketful of rocks bring home
So, brothers, don't you cry!

      Chorus: Oh, California,
                   That's the land for me!
                   I'm bound for San Francisco
                   With my washbowl on my knee!

TRADITIONAL – 1848

The Beverly version of *I Come From Salem City* is called *The San Francisco Company* and also sung to the tune *Oh! Susanna*. The lyrics are from the *Bark San Francisco's* log journal, currently on display at Historic Beverly, in Beverly Massachusetts. [6]

The California Gold Diggers

The California Gold Diggers [7] was found in the Lester S. Levy Sheet Music Collection at The Sheridan Libraries & University Museums, Johns Hopkins University. Jesse Hutchinson, leader of the Hutchinson family singing group of Lynn, Massachusetts composed this song in 1849, borrowing portions of the melody *Dan Emmett (Boatman Dance)* for the refrain. Irwin Silber says in the *Songs of the Great American West* that this piece became the "unofficial anthem for many a gold-hunting band." [8] Several versions of this song have survived through a process where "American sailors whittle down the words, changed and re-changed and spliced the tune with another, added a call and response pattern to the verse and created one of the great sea chanteys of our literature." [8]

Henry A. Tuttle recorded a version of *The California Gold Diggers* called *Ho! Boys Ho!* in the *Bark La Grange's* passenger log journal #621. When the bark left Salem for San Francisco on Saturday, March 17, 1849 at 4 P.M., Tuttle wrote:

*The California Gold Digger*s courtesy of Lester S. Levy Collection of Sheet Music, Sheridan Libraries, Johns Hopkins University

> All things being in readiness for sailing, dense masses have congregated on the wharf to witness our departure. Friends and acquaintances witnessed as our vessel swung by her stern fast impatiently waiting to be freed. The Barker family came forward and sang a song, which called forth shouts and applause in good old fashion style three times three. After which the pilot gave orders to let go and we were off with a fine breeze from the northward, which soon carried us out of hauling distance. And we bid farewell to good old Salem for the term of two years, perhaps forever. 5 P.M. the pilot left us and we gave our guides in the pilot boat three cheers while we moved along with a light breeze in good spirits. [9]

The Californian [10] is another version of *The California Gold Diggers* from log journal #1001 also kept on board the *Bark La Grange* by journal keeper A.E. Kitfield. The log details the voyage from Salem to San Francisco from March 1849 to August 1850. After leaving Salem Harbor, Kitfield wrote:

March 17, 1849 P.M.

> Sailed from India Wharf for San Francisco. Thousands assembled to see us sail among whom were Barker, Hutchinson & Beasmey that gave us a song in the time of the dance the *Boatman Dance*; of course a very pleasant sensation comes over us all. We had a light breeze, southwest. Through the night, slept pretty well---

March 18, Sabbath Morning

> Came on deck winds out Northeast rather a light breeze, spent the day much more pleasantly then I anticipated. Some ten or twelve of us gathered on the quarter deck and sung from the *Carmina Sacral*.[11] Mr. Bogardens with his bass viol and Mr. French with his violin made it sound pretty nice. In the course of the day we could see almost all hands engaged in reading something. Some with their bibles some with newspapers, some with words. While some few were feeding the inhabitants of the sea with what they had to eat, as it did not suit their stomach. Finally the day lapsed very well.[10]

Journal keeper, William F. Morgan wrote down even another version called *The California Song* in the *Bark La Grange's* passenger log journal #1702. Morgan confirms that *The California Song* was "written by Jess Hutchinson and sung by him and the Barker Family on the departure of the Salem and California Mining and Trading Expedition, March the 17, 1849." [12]

The California Gold Diggers

> We've formed our band, and we're all well manned,
> To journey afar to the promised land,
> Where the golden ore is rich in store,
> On the banks of the Sacramento shore.
>
> Chorus: Then, Ho! Boys Ho! To California go;
> There's plenty of gold in the world we're told,
> On the banks of the Sacramento.
> Heigh ho and away we go,
> Digging up gold in Frisco.

As off we roam through the dark sea foam,
We'll never forget kind friends at home,
But memory kind will bring to mind,
The love of those we've left behind.

Chorus: Then, Ho! Boys Ho! To California go;
           There's plenty of gold in the world we're told,
           On the banks of the Sacramento.
           Heigh ho and away we go,
           Digging up gold in Frisco.

We expect our share of the coarsest fare,
And sometimes sleep in the open air,
On the cold damp ground we'll all sleep sound,
Except when the wolves come howling 'round.

Chorus: Then, Ho! Boys Ho! To California go;
           There's plenty of gold in the world we're told,
           On the banks of the Sacramento.
           Heigh ho and away we go,
           Digging up gold in Frisco.

As we explore the distant shore,
We'll fill our pockets with the shining ore,
And how 'twill sound as the wind goes 'round,
Of our picking up gold by the "dozen pound."

Chorus: Then, Ho! Boys Ho! To California go;
           There's plenty of gold in the world we're told,
           On the banks of the Sacramento.
           Heigh ho and away we go,
           Digging up gold in Frisco.

O, the gold is thar most any whar,
They dig it out with an iron bar,
And where it's thick, with a spade and pick,
They've taken out lumps as "big as a brick!"

Chorus: Then, Ho! Boys Ho! To California go;
          There's plenty of gold in the world we're told
          On the banks of the Sacramento.
          Heigh ho and away we go,
          Digging up gold in Frisco.

JESSE HUTCHISON, JR. – 1849

The Hoodah Day Shanty more commonly known, as *Banks Of Sacramento* seems to be a composite of and derived from the Hutchinson song *The California Gold Diggers*. Over time, the melody changed to *Camptown Races* also written by Stephen Foster[13] with the pattern of the verses being followed by the refrain, A Hoo-dah, A Hoo-dah. William Main Doerflinger who wrote *Songs of the Sailor and Lumberman* supports this view stating, "Tune and short refrains of Foster's song are combined in the shanty with the chorus of one introduced by the Hutchinson Family." [14] Two other Salem connected versions that show the transformation of the song are Frederick P. Harlow's *Banks Of Sacramento* found in *The Making of a Sailor* and Captain Edward B. Trumbull's version called *Hoodah Day Shanty* included in James Madison Carpenter's doctorate thesis entitled *Forecastle Songs and Chanties*.

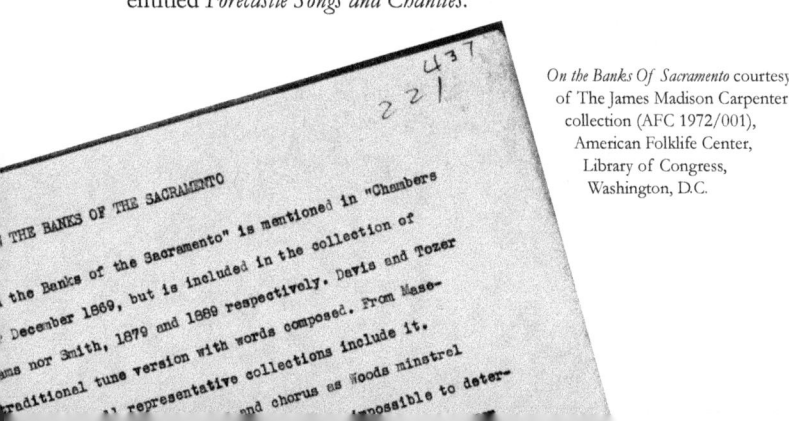

On the Banks Of Sacramento courtesy of The James Madison Carpenter collection (AFC 1972/001), American Folklife Center, Library of Congress, Washington, D.C.

I've Been Dreamin'

Bill Adams wrote the song *I've Been Dreamin'*. The song was published in *Songs of the Sea and Sailors' Chanteys* edited by Robert Frothingham. [15] Adams is longing for the romantic days of old on a clipper ship going westward from Salem to California, singing and hoisting the topsails as referenced in these two lines:

> I wants them lights by Frisco, an' lights by Salem too,
> An' dandy skippers swearin' at the singin' of the crew.

I've Been Dreamin'

I've been dreamin', Of a randy, dandy clipper with her tops'ls set,
Pitchin' heavy down the westin' with the leeches wet.
Bill Newland, the old skipper, from his high bridge head,
Shoutin' to us packet rats — an' these the words he said:

"Hop along, now! Loose them 'gallants! Skip aloft, now! Jump along!"
Oh, them packet rats were swearin' an' a-breakin' into song!
Packet rats a-roarin', "Ranzo," rats a-singin' "Roll an' Go,"
Haulin' on them 'gallant braces, cryin', "Blow, boys, blow!"

> Let her blow for Frisco city!
> Let the dandy clipper race!
> For them swingin' feet an' pretty
> Of the gals at Tony's place.
>
> Soon we'll see old Tony smilin',
> Hear his girls begin to sing,
> Hear old Billy Dick beguilin'
> Music from a fiddle-string!

Off To California

    Oh, there's drowned an' perished clippers
    An' there's rats that died —
    But there's gals wi' flowered slippers
    An' their skirts flung wide!

Did you say there are no clippers? Did you say them days is done?
Days of packet rats an' packets, an' stars an' moon an' sun?
O' lights upon the water, a-shinin' on the sea?
My God, but I'm a packet rat! What will become of me?

I've got to see tall clippers, I've got to sing an' shout
When the 'gallants are mastheaded and the jibs are runnin' out.
I've got to roar "Ranzo" an' "Blow, my bullies, blow!"
When the ice-cakes heap a-cracklin', an' the Horn is lost in snow.

I wants them lights by Frisco, an' lights by Salem too,
An' dandy skippers swearin' at the singin' of the crew.
Red Jacket's gone? And Dancing Wave? Guidin' Star as well?
Then what of Golden Era? . . . God help me! This is hell!

Good-by, farewell, kedge anchor! The shoals lie deep about;
The packet rats are singin', an' their chorus dyin' out.
The clippers lie a-wastin' where the westin' sun burns red,
An' the packet rats are restin' in the havens of the dead.

Good-be to Dame Romancing an' her dainty feathered frock!
Good-by to all the laughter at the swingin' of the lock!
Good-by to capstan payments, good-by to ships at sea —
If the packets rest a-westin' — ah — westin's right for me!

                            BILL ADAMS – 1924

Witch of the Wave

Several ships left Salem in the 1850s for California to transport gold seekers, carry supplies and some to continue on to far off ports. Several clipper ships like *Witchcraft*, *John Bertram*, and *Witch of the Wave* all with a Salem connection were headed west. The *Witchcraft*, captained by William C. Rodgers who was born in Salem in 1823, was one of the first clipper ships to head for California. Rodgers "acquired the knowledge of seamanship and navigation that enabled him to become one of the most famous among the youngest clipper ship captains." The *John Bertram* was another clipper ship from Salem that left for California in 1850. "She was named for Captain Bertram, one of Salem's most famous sea captains and merchants." [16] The commander of the *John Bertram* was Captain Lordholm.

The *Witch of the Wave*, built in 1851, and was launched from Portsmouth, New Hampshire. The ship was owned by John Bertram and Alfred Peabody of Salem. After launching, she headed to Salem to "obtain her register." The ballad *Witch of the Wave* was discovered in Arthur Clark's *The Clipper Ship Era, 1843 - 1869*. He recounted, "As the Witch of the Wave rounded Thatcher Island," it was said to Captain Bertram that

Salem Gazette, March 27, 1849, courtesy of Christine Elizabeth Mistretta's Private Collection

"perhaps he thought it be a good plan to set some sail," to see what effect some canvas would have on the new clipper.[16] Jonathan Nicholas, of Salem, recited the following impromptu lines to celebrate the ship's inspection.

> I wonder what's the dreadful row,
> They're kicking up in Portsmouth now!
> The people running up and down,
> Crying 'All Salem's come to town!'
>
> > Chorus: Clear the track, the ship is starting!
> > Clear the track, the ship is starting!
> > Clear the track, the ship is starting!
> > And Portsmouth hearts are sad at parting.
>
> They say a man came down to-day,
> To carry the Witch of the Wave away;
> And the people think he ought n't oughter,
> Just because he's been and brought her.
>
> They called it rainy yesterday,
> But I know better, anyway;
> 'T was only Portsmouth people crying,
> To see the good ship's colors flying!
>
> But Captain B. said, 'Hang the sorrow!
> The sun is bound to shine to-morrow.'
> And when he speaks it's no use talking—
> So the clouds and the blues, they took to walking.
>
> And so to-day the sun shines bright,
> And Salem sends her heart's delight;
> And the good ship flies, and the wind blows free,
> As she leaps to her lover's arms—the sea!

They have crowded her deck with the witty and wise,
The saltest wisdom and merriest eyes;
And manned her yards with a gallant crew,
That it tickles her staunch old ribs to view.

They say she's bound to sail so fast,
That a man on deck can't catch the mast!
And a porpoise trying to keep ahead,
Will get run over and killed stone dead.

Then here's a health to the hands that wrought her,
And three times three to the mind that thought her,
For thought's the impulse, work's the way,
That brings all Salem here to-day.

>Chorus: Clear the track, the ship is starting!
>Clear the track, the ship is starting!
>Clear the track, the ship is starting!
>And Portsmouth hearts are sad at parting.

TRADITIONAL – 1850

Captain John Bertram was born on the Channel Island of Jersey (off the coast of France) in 1796 and his family moved to Salem in 1807. Starting as a cabin boy at age 16, he eventually earned promotion to captain. His career as merchant and ship owner was long. He principally traded in South American for rubber and hides, Zanzibar for gum copal, ivory, coffee and spices, and California supplying goods for the gold rush.

Bertram lived all his life in Salem, dying there on March 22, 1882 and laid to in rest Harmony Grove Cemetery. Among his many charitable acts he founded the Bertram Home for Aged Men on Salem Common and left his family home to the city for the public library. Originally built in 1855, the mansion at 370 Essex Street was built in the Italianate style of brick and brownstone. [17] Captain Bertram flew his trademark red and white flag on each of his ships. To this day, the red and white flowers planted around the library fountain symbolize Bertram's colors.

Bertram's House, now the Salem Public Library, courtesy of Mary Barker

Witch of the Wave (tune)

Witch of the Wave can be found in several tune books including Ralph Sweet's *Fifer's Delight* and William Bradbury *Ryan's Mammoth Collection*.[18] The Library of Congress website has a different, old-time tune also called *Witch of the Wave* played by Henry Reed of Virginia and transcribed by Alan Jabbour. The connection to both Bertram's ship, *Witch of the Wave* and Salem is only speculative but it makes sense to note the tune in this book.

TRADITIONAL – 1800s

Off To California

Gold

Log keeper William F. Morgan recorded *Gold* [19] in the *Bark La Grange* log journal #1702 on Wednesday October 24, 1849.

Cursed be the gold and silver which persuade,
Weak men to follow far fatiguing trade,
The lily peace outshines the silver store,
And life is dearer then the golden ore;

But money tempts us over the desert brown,
To every distant dime and wealthy town,
How oft we tempt the land, and oft the sea;
And are we only yet unpaid by thee?

Ah! Why was ruin so attractive made?
Or why fond men so easily betrayed?
Why need we not, whilst mad we haste along,
The gentle voice of peace or pleasant songs,

Or wherefore think, the flowery mountains side,
The fountain murmurs, And the valley forbid(e).
Why think we these left pleasing to behold
Shine dreary deserts, if they lead to gold.

TRADITIONAL – 1849

The Gold Hunter's Story

The Gold Hunter's Story [20] was found in the *Bark La Grange's* journal log #1702. Log keeper William F. Morgan wrote that Chat Hunt of Washington City penned the song in 1849.

    Gold Hunters listen unto me,
    A story all relate
    Which Happened on board the Tahmaroo,
    On her voyage round the Cape;
    Down in the second cabin,
    They ate all kinds of stuff.
    I always chewed the harder,
    When I got my heavy duff.

Chorus: Oh that heavy duff
           I never got enough
           Some lone salt pork and dunderfunk
           But I rather have my duff.

    They sent a chunk on each men's plate,
    I wish they'd give me more
    It taste a little sight better
    Than dumplings hard ashore
    Then up on deck I travel
    Like the lasses from my (thoughts)
    And wait with all jobs patience,
    For the next duff day to come.

Chorus: Oh that heavy duff
           I never got enough
           Some lone salt pork and dunderfunk
           But I rather have my duff.

Off To California

Down in the second cabin,
Where the beams they lay so low
The bed bugs in the blanket lay
And the rats they sleep below.
Oh there is the spot
Where the duff it taste so sweet
And when the steward rings the bell,
We tumble down to eat.

Chorus: Oh that heavy duff
        I never got enough
        Some lone salt pork and dunderfunk
        But I rather have my duff.

Down in the second cabin,
I've sat for many an hour
And the smell of pork and beans
And hard bread rather sour;
Oh how heavy duff
I mourned when thou departed
I gave my life a farewell snack,
And upon decks I started.

Chorus: Oh that heavy duff
        I never got enough
        Some lone salt pork and dunderfunk
        But I rather have my duff.

CHAT HUNT – 1849

The Returned Californian

Found in the website of the Library of Congress, *The Returned Californian* [21] was written by James Pierpont and published in 1852. Pierpont is best known for writing *Jingle Bells* but he wrote this song based on his experiences during the California gold rush and the failure of his San Francisco business.

The piece was published in Boston by E. H. Wade and was written expressly for *Ordway's Aeolians*, a local minstrel group. John Pond Ordway of Salem arranged the music for which S. C. Howard was the vocalist. Ordway, born August 1, 1824 was a doctor, composer, music entrepreneur and politician. He and his father left Salem in the mid 1840s, moved to Boston where they opened a music store. Well-known bandleader Patrick Gilmore, who lived in Salem for a few years, worked in Ordway's store in Boston and appeared with the Aeolians. [22] As an interesting note, Gilmore led the *Salem Cadet Band* and wrote several tunes including the *Salem Hornpipe* and towards the end of the Civil War he wrote *When Johnny Comes Marching Home*. Both pieces are referenced in *Old Salem in Ballad and Song*.

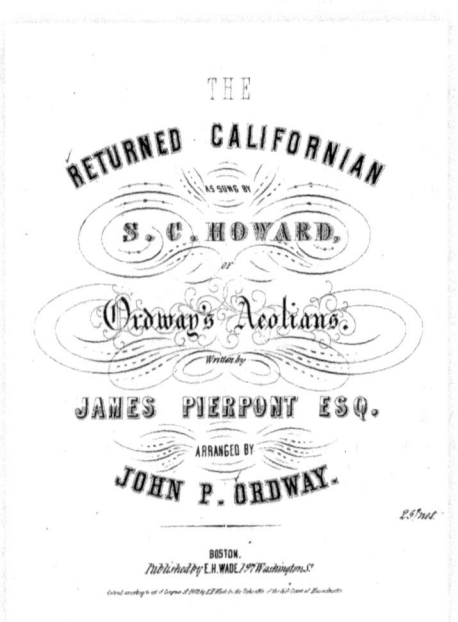

The Returned Californian, courtesy of the Sheet Music Division of the Library of Congress

The Returned Californian

Oh, I'm going far away from my Creditors just now,
I ain't the tin to pay 'em and they're kicking up a row;
I ain't one of those lucky ones that works for 'Uncle Sam,'
There's no chance for speculation and the mines ain't worth a Copper.

There's my tailor vowing vengeance and he swears he'll give me Fits,
And Sheriff's running after me with pockets full of writs;
And which ever way I turn, I am sure to meet a dun,
So I guess the best thing I can do, is just to cut and run.

Oh! I wish those 'tarnel critters that wrote home about the gold
Were in the place the Scriptures say 'is never very cold;'
For they told about the heaps of dust and lumps so mighty big,
But they never said a single word how hard they were to dig.

So I went up to the mines and I helped to turn a stream,
And got trusted on the strength of that delusive golden dream;
But when we got to digging we found 'twas all a sham,
And we who dam'd the rivers by our creditors were damn'd.

Oh! I'm going far away but I don't know where I'll go,
I oughter travel homeward but they'll laugh at me I know;
For I told 'em when I started I was bound to make a pile,
But if they could only see mine now I rather guess they'd smile.

If of these United States I was the President,
No man that owed another should ever pay a cent;
And he who dunn'd another should be banished far away,
And attention to the pretty girls is all a man should pay.

JAMES PIERPONT – 1852

ON THE ROAD TO SAL[EM]

COMPOSED and DEDICATED

to the

FIELD and STAFF Officers of the 4th Light Infantry Regim[ent]
Volunteer Militia, and to the Officers and Members of the CA[...]
who marched from Boston to Salem Aug. 23rd 18[..]
accompanied by the

BOSTON BRIGADE BAND.

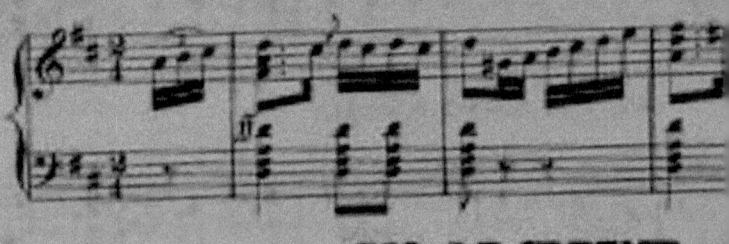

COL. J. D. GREENE.

~ 2 ~
Superstition

The Mermaid

The sighting of a mermaid is considered an omen of bad luck that dates back to Homer's *Odyssey*. *The Mermaid* could be sung as a capstan shanty while the crew on a sailing ship walked in rhythm to raise the anchor. The ballad dates back to the 1700s and can be found in numerous folk music books. A version is printed in Francis Child's *English and Scottish Popular Ballads*, Child Ballad #289.[1] Child's variant or version A is titled *The Seaman's Distress*. His variant B, *The Stormy Winds Do Blow*, is from Chappell's, *Popular Music of the Olden Time*.[2] Each variant follows the same story line while slightly changing the words and usually sung to a different tune.

The singer can change the names of the towns mentioned in the song to suit the port of call. The mentioning of Salem was used in several versions one of which was recorded by traditional singer, Paul Clayton's on his LP called *Whaling And Sailing Songs*[3] and another by folk singer, David Jones on his CD called *Widdecombe Fair*. In Bertrand Harris's collection, *The Traditional Tunes of the Child Ballads, Volume 4*, he cited three sources that mentioned Salem in the lyrics:

A. Sung by Bascom Lamar Lunsford in Washington DC 1949 LC/AAFS No. 9476 B3
B. Sung by A.J. Ford, Crandon, Wisconsin 1937 LC/AAFS No. 2236 A1
C. Sung by Elizabeth Walker Ford, Central Valley, California September 26, 1962 LC/AAFS No. 11,223 A3. Collected by Sidney Robertson Cowell[4]

Superstition

The Mermaid

Twas Friday morn when we set sail,
And we had not got far from the land:
When the Captain, he spied a lovely mermaid,
With a comb and a glass in her hand

> Chorus: Oh the ocean's waves will roll,
> And the stormy winds will blow;
> While we poor sailors go skipping aloft
> And the landlubbers lie down below, below, below
> And the landlubbers lie down below

Then up spoke the Captain of our gallant ship,
And a well-spoken man was he;
"I have me a wife in Salem town,
And tonight a widow will be."

> Chorus: Oh the ocean's waves will roll,
> And the stormy winds will blow;
> While we poor sailors go skipping aloft
> And the landlubbers lie down below, below, below
> And the landlubbers lie down below.

And up spoke the Cook of our gallant ship,
And a greasy old Cook was he;
"I care much more for my kettles and my pots,
Than I do for the bottom of the sea."

Chorus: Oh the ocean's waves will roll,
             And the stormy winds will blow,
             While we poor sailors go skipping aloft
             And the landlubbers lie down below, below, below
             And the landlubbers lie down below.

Then up spoke the Cabin boy, of our gallant ship,
And a dirty little brat was he;
"I have friends in Boston town,
That don't care a ha' penny for me."

Chorus: Oh the ocean's waves will roll,
             And the stormy winds will blow;
             While we poor sailors go skipping aloft
             And the landlubbers lie down below, below, below
             And the landlubbers lie down below.

Then three times 'round went our gallant ship,
And three times 'round went she;
And the third time that she went 'round;
She sank to the bottom of the sea.

Chorus: Oh the ocean's waves will roll,
             And the stormy winds will blow,
             While we poor sailors go skipping aloft
             And the landlubbers lie down below, below, below
             And the landlubbers lie down below.

TRADITIONAL – 1700'S

Of the Lost Ship

Eugene Richard White wrote *Of The Lost Ship*[5] in 1897. The song's refrain repeats after each verse saying, "Fell through a crack in the floor of the sea." The loss of the *Schooner Kite*, out of Baltimore, is a mystery to many folks on shore. White and his connection to Salem are vague except for one reference, the mentioning of "Salem Folk" in his song.

White died at the age of 36 and all his written work was found tucked away in his desk drawers and boxes. Harry Persons Taber wrote in memory of White:

> Born far inland, the sea was not his, except through some subtle influence planted generations before. He even never saw the great blue sea save from the shore where it had been calmed by the touch of men; yet he breathes in some of his songs the spirit of the vastness and the beauty and the glory, which must have been known to the men of whom he writes.[5]

It is interesting how White can write about the sea without living on or near the ocean.

Of The Lost Ship

WHAT has become of the good ship Kite?
Where is her hull of chosen oak?
Who were the Victors, what the Fight?
    The old Wives—whom did they invoke,
That should tell them so uncannily:

"Fell through a crack in the Floor of the Sea"?

"Trafficked with death in a cruise fore-done,"
    The Preachers drone to the Salem Folk,
When the Sea has swallowed up the Sun
    And the white gulls glint—was it they who spoke?
Wes'-Sou'-West from the Devil's Quay:

"Fell through a crack in the Floor of the Sea"?

Of the old-time Band there's not a man
    Who has ever told how the ship went down.
Were they marked by God with the fear-some ban?
    Butchered they priests in a sun-white town?
Do they harry Hell where they may be:

"Fell through a crack in the Floor of the Sea"?

Though ye searched the West to the guttering sun,
    Or the East till the baffled lights burn black,
Or North to the bergs till the South be won,
    The changeling shadows answer back,
And their trembling lips pale piteously:

"Fell through a crack in the Floor of the Sea"?

And when the great grim Finger becks
    The whining Seas from their ancient bed,
Shall some tongue speak from the world-old wrecks
    To read the log of the Thwarted Dead?
Is there never an end on the mystery:

"Fell through a crack in the Floor of the Sea"?

                            EUGENE RICHARD WHITE – 1897

Superstition

The Gosport
or The Ship's Carpenter

Francis Boardman recorded *The Gosport* [6] in the *Vaughan's* logbook #1057. The *Vaughan* sailed out of Salem in 1767 on a voyage to Jamaica then on to London. The ballad is also called *The Daemon Lover* and *The Cruel Ship's Carpenter*. [7] This ballad tells a story of a ship's carpenter who, upon learning his lover was pregnant, "led her through groves and valleys so deep," to kill and bury her in a shallow grave. In some versions of this ballad the woman comes back to haunt the ship's carpenter. In Boardman's version, she does not.

According to the *Penguin Book of Canadian Folk Songs*, *The Ship's Carpenter* is based on the ballad *Gosport Tragedy*, printed in London circa 1750. Its 35 verses were condensed into an eleven-stanza broadside, called *The Cruel Ship's Carpenter*, which was very popular in Canada, England and the US around the 1900s. It seems to be a source for *Pretty Polly* and is certainly related to many of the other murder ballads. [8] *The Gosport* is also found in the books, *The Ships and Sailors of Old Salem and Songs the Whalemen Sang.* [9]

The Gosport

In Gosport of late there a Damsel did dwell,
For wit and for beauty did she many excel.

A young man he courted her to be his dear,
And by his trade was a Ship Carpenter.

He sees my dear Molly if you will agree,
And will then consent for to marry me.

Your love it will ease me of sorrow and care,
If you will but marry a ship carpenter.

With blushes more charming then roses in June,
She answers Sweet William for to wed I am too young.

Young men they are fickle and so very vain,
If a maid she is kind they will quickly distain.

The most beautiful woman that ever was born,
When a man has ensnared her beauty he scorns.

O my dear Molly what makes you say so,
The beauty is the Haven to which I will go.

If you will consent for the Church for to steer,
There I will cast anchor and stay with my dear.

I more shall beside with the charms of thy love,
This love is as true as the true Turtle Dove.

All that I do crave is to marry my dear,
And enter we in marriage no dangers we will fear.

She the life of a virgin Sweet William I prize,
For marrying brings trouble and sorrow like wise.

But all was in vane then his suite she did denied,
Yet he did persuade her for love to Comply.

And by his cunning her heart did betray,
And with too (lude) desire he led her astray.

This past on a while and at length you will hear,
The King wanted sailors and to sea he must steer.

This grieved the fare Damsel almost to the heart,
To think of her true love so soon she must part.

She sees my dear will as you go to sea,
Remember the vows that you made unto me.

With the kindest expressions he to her did say,
I will marry my Molly and I go away.

That means tomorrow to me you will come,
Then we will be married and our love carried on.

With the kindest embraces they parted that night,
She went for to meet him next morning by light.

He sees my dear charmer you must go with me,
Before we are married a friend for to see.

He led her through groves and valleys so deep,
That this fare damsel began for to weep.

She sees my dear William you lead me astray,
On purpose my innocent life to be betray.

He those are true words and none can you save,
For all this whole night I have been digging your grave.

A spade standing by and a grave there she see,
But oh must this grave be a bride bed to me.

TRADITIONAL – 1767

~ 3 ~
Ship and Prison Logbooks

Hills of Georgetown

The Hills of Georgetown was recorded by log keeper, William F. Morgan on Sunday May 27 in 1850 on the *Bark La Grange* while on its way to California. Morgan wrote, "We have been in Georgetown (Bahamas) a week now but shall move soon over to the middle fork and then lose the delightful prospects which attracts the eye at every turn among the hills of Georgetown." [1]

It's a beautiful scene with its hill of green
    That I see at the close of day.

With its waters so bright that like liquid light
    They seem in the breeze to play.

There the setting sun 'ere his march is done
    Poured fourth such an amber stream.

That the gorgeous hills and the laughing rills
    Were rich for the poets themes.

And over my head such a dome is spread
    Made life of the threads of light.

From the trailing becomes of the sun's last gleams
    That it seems for earth to bright.

It is sweet we know that she soul shall go
    From its home on the pleasant earth.

From a scene like this to the helms of bliss
    Where all that is fair has birth.

> To ask for a shroud, but a shinning cloud
> From the depths of the .... seas.
>
> And an angel guide to the portal wide
> What may be enclosed to me.
>
> WILLIAM F. MORGAN, LOG KEEPER – 1850

Lines composed on a
Court Martial of Oliver Poland
for the theft on board The America

Lines Composed on a Court Martial of Oliver Poland was discovered in the logbook of the ship *The America*. The piece detailed a privateering voyage from homeport Salem into the Atlantic Ocean, beginning Monday, September 7, 1812. The ship belonged to the fabulously successful privateer George Crowninshield and sailed under the steady command of Captain Joseph Ropes. James Cheever, the log keeper wrote, as the *The America* left Salem harbor:

> Commence with gentle breezes and plain weather at 10 P.M. got underway with the wind at East/Southeast in the good ship America. Joseph Ropes master bound on a cruise. At meridian sailed past Bakers Island out in the offing Captain Crowninshield left us. So ends harbor sail. [2]

The breezes were not always gentle. Further on during the journey, a sailor was caught stealing, hence, a court martial and the song.

35

Lines Composed on a Court Martial of Oliver Poland

This court comprised of men of knowledge,
And genius: tho not been at College.

Cheever, Wedger, Haggot and Brown,
Whose firm integrity now will be known.

Their minds being well on justice bent,
Aft on the Lee poop they were sent.

Where they debate upon the cause,
Govern'd by their country's laws.

They try the culprit, find him guilty,
Of theft; a crime both mean and filthy.

Of entering into illicit trade,
And stealing shoes already made.

From a Marine too whose clothes were few,
A sea convict he fulfills too.

His shipmates therefore he ....
In consequence he must take one dozen.

The Judge announces the just sentence,
And many stripes produce resistance.

The Boatswain pipes all hands to muster.

JAMES CHEEVER, LOG KEEPER – 1812

The Sailor's Early Home

The Sailor's Early Home was found in the *Bark La Grange Passenger's Journal* in 1849.[3] The journal keeper was Henry A. Tuttle of Salem. It is likely Tuttle copied the ballad from a printed version that he had in his possession since the spelling was accurate and no lines were changed or omitted. Further research indicates that Rev. S. D. Phelps wrote *The Sailor's Early Home* found in the *Union Fifth Reader: Embracing a Full Exposition of the Principles of Rhetorical Reading.*[4]

Away, away o'er the dashing spray,
May bark speeds light and free;
And the piping gale, through the straining sail,
Whistles loud in its merry glee;
And the stars at night, with luster bright,
Shine out o'er the vast expanse;
And the moon from her throne on high looks down
On the restless billow's dance.

There's charm in the eye when the waves leap high,
And a music in their roar;
And the stars, as they shine in their spheres divine,
A joy on the spirits pour.
But the sea in its might,
 And the stars with their light,
That glance on the crested foam,
Can not make me gay; for my thoughts are away.
In my childhood's early home.

And dreams come fat of the blissful past,
Ere my heart had felt or known;
The ills of life, and the cares and strife
That oppress and weigh it down;
Or experience, bought by suffering, taught
The lesson sad and drear,
That each sparkling joy finds its sad alloy,
And hope is chilled by fear.

In a quiet nook, by a gentle brook,
Stands that home to memory dear;
And the purling steam,
As it glides in the beam
Of the sun, shines bright and clear.
I am there again with a happy train,
The same who in other years
Held their festive play with spirits gay,
And eyes undimmed by tears.

Those years as they passed have shadows cat,
On them, as they have on me;
And none remain who swelled the train
Of joy 'neath the household tree.
And I weep as the thought with sadness fraught
Settles dark on my troubled brain,
That the bliss I proved and the friends I loved
Shall never be mine again.

To the church-yard nigh,
Where the wild winds sigh;
With a low and mournful tone,
And the peaceful rest of earth's tranquil breast,
The cherished ones are gone.

There, clustering round, in that hallowed ground,
Affection's tablets stand;
And the last stone reared on that spot endeared
Was raised by my trembling hand.

Away, far away, o'er the dashing spray,
My bark bears me fast and free;
And my destiny lies under other skies
Than those so beloved by me.
And downward apace o'er my storm-beaten face,
Tears fall like the summer rain,
As my thoughts wander back from my ocean track
To the home I shall ne'er see again.

REV. S. D. PHELPS – 1840s

Of Dartmore (sic) Prison

Joseph Valpey, Jr. of Salem was one of thousands of Americans captured by the British Navy during the War of 1812 and sent to languish in Dartmoor Prison in Devon, England. He kept a prison logbook recounting daily activities, the people with whom he spoke, and recorded the conditions and events at the prison. He had shipped out of Boston with a Letter of Marque on the schooner *Monkey* on November 2, 1813 at the height of hostilities. Under Master John Glover the ship was trying for Charleston, South Carolina.[5] The ship was soon captured and the men were sent to Dartmoor located in the dismal plains of Princetown. The prison was designed and built by Daniel Asher Alexander and constructed between 1806 and 1809 by local labor to hold between 6,000 and 7,000 prisoners of the Napoleonic Wars and American prisoners from the War of 1812.[6] Valpey wrote in the song, *Of Dartmore Prison*:

Of Dartmore Prison

Of Dartmore Prison I'll tel(l) all I can,
Describe the condition of ten thousand men.
There manner of pastime and how they all are,
Describe these fine buildings and how we all fare.

On top of a mountain those prisons does stand,
A place pich' on purpose for tormenting man.
Where Frenchmen and yankey's together must stay,
Until the war's o'er or else run away.

Our manner of living depends very bad,
Not grub half enough every countenance sad.
Nor clothing sufficient to cover our skin,
And no more indulgence we get from the King.

Our manner of pastime its hard to explain,
But Keeno and dice is our principal game.
While some set at drinking together they sing,
Bad luck to the prison short life to the King.

Now place all together of what I relate,
And had I not reason's for to god dam'n my fate.
But I bear it with patience and cheerfully sing,
Long life to our President and a curse on the King.

JOSEPH VALPEY, JR – 1814

Hunting for Lice and Fleas [7]

Valpey spent more than a year and a half at the Dartmoor Prison. Days were long in prison and somewhat boring. He observed other inmates passing the time hunting for lice and fleas. Valpey found humor in writing a song about the pursuit.

> In yellow dress from head to foot,
> Just like a swarm of bees.
> From morn to night you'll see a sight,
> Of hunting lice and fleas.
>
> They skip and crawl most ravingly,
> And pass from man to man.
> If they could speak you'd hear them say,
> Now catch me if you can.
>
> The other Morn as I walked out,
> To take the pleasant air.
> I saw a Louse whose magnitude,
> With horror he made me stare.
>
> Old Trafalgar he pind him fast,
> And killed him for the crime.
> Saying yesterday was yours my Louse,
> But now the day is mine.

JOSEPH VALPEY, JR – 1814

The Fruits of Gambling's

From the spring of 1813 until March 1815 about 6,500 American sailors were imprisoned at Dartmoor. These were naval prisoners and impressed American seamen discharged from British vessels. Even though the British were in charge of the prison, the prisoners created their own governance and culture. They had courts, which doled out punishments, a prison market, a theater and a gambling room. [8] Valpey wrote in the song, *The Fruits of Gambling's* [9] about its dangers and how it can lead to a troubled life.

> Come fellow prisoner's one and all,
> To reason lend an ear.
> To keep up gambling as you do,
> Your ruin'd men its clear.
>
> For reason first should Beasly* hear,
> How we this money use'd.
> He d say the prisoner's was to blame,
> They that the states abus'd.
>
> The money that's sent was for intent,
> To help us in this place.
> Instead of which you all must see,
> It clothes you in disgrace.
>
> For should you ask for any more,
> As each man ought to do.
> Then would your Injured Country say,
> No money more for you.

For reason why when I advance,
To you this trifling sum.
You keep up gambling night and day,
Which hurts you every one.

Yet a few it help's a little while,
But mark his latter end.
His bank gets broke, his dunnage sold,
This Man's without a friend.

Then stealing next is there intent,
Which often time's you see.
Then be seized up like any dog,
And flogged he must be.

This story's told when he gets home,
Unto his friends or wife.
This man's dispised by them he loved,
Therefore he cannot value life.

To now avoid those ills I've stated,
From gambling now refrain.
Then you'll be helped and respected,
Should you ever get home again.

JOSEPH VALPEY, JR – 1814

Ship Bengal at Sea

This song is from the *Bengal's* whaling journals and account books dated 1832 – 1835. [10] The log keeper, William Silver details a round trip voyage to Oceania and then back to its homeport in Salem lasting from March 1832 to February 1835. The ship's owners were among the leading merchants in Salem, Pickering Dodge, Benjamin Pickman, and Joseph Peabody. When the *Bengal* was in its homeport, local recruiting agents placed ads in the *Salem Gazette* looking for "men whose instincts are to follow the sea."

Salem Gazette, March 9, 1832, advertisement selling whale oil on Union Wharf and *Salem Gazette*, March 6, 1832, 25 young men wanted for whaling on the ship *Bengal*

Ship Bengal at Sea

Oh say shall the morn's early guide,
Waft me from the arms of my love home,
Or say am I yet to bewail,
Misfortune has caused me to roam.

Oh say must I and these fond loving,
Does misfortune her (guest) over flow,
Oh adorned we in sympathetic showers,
Yes love I must bid you adieu.

With care have I tested life charms,
On the bosom of friendship and love,
But now I am forced from thin arms,
The wide bellowing ocean to roam

The sun spreads his lucid lucid way,
While the tune that is sung of heave ho!
Over anchor is lone short and away
I come love to bid you adieu.

The day dawns in the east,
The landscape or twilight in view,
The breeze gently blows from the west,
It blows love to bear me from you.

When trumpets I am test to and fro,
Or in storms I am lifted from you.
One thought on your breast may it dwell,
For the one that now bids you adieu.

Adieu to columbines in (proud) fields,
Adieu to the daughters she love,
And adieu to the sun that now yields,
And adieu to humanity shore.

Our canvas is spread to the shore,
Our signals are moving in mind,
Love I am hurried away to the seas,
Our emblem of love fare you well.

The Greenland Whale

The Greenland Whale[10] is another song recorded by William Silver but he did not give it a title.[11] It can be found in the book *Songs the Whalemen Sang*,[12] which was first collected by Gale Huntington from the 1833 *Bengal* journal. He lists many names including *The Whale*, *The Greenland Whale Fishery* and *The Whale Catcher*. Huntington ended up calling the song *The Greenland Whale* in his book., A local shanty group, *Starboard List* living on the North Shore in the 1970s, performed the ballad at the Salem Bicentennial and recorded two LPs, *Songs of the Tall Ships* & *Cruising 'Round Yarmouth*.[13] The group included Charles O'Hegarty, David Jones, and Peter Marston. Their re-released CD *Starboard List* included a version of *The Greenland Whale* called *Greenland Whale Fisheries*. Peter still attends the local shanty sings on Monday evenings in Gloucester, Massachusetts.

The Salem Bicentennial Commission Invites the City of Salem and its Neighbors to an Open House Festival at Salem's Two Great Museums Saturday & Sunday, June 7 & 8

The Greenland Whale

It was seventeen hundred and eighty-four
On March the seventeenth day
We weighed our anchor to our bow

  And for Greenland bore away, brave boys
  And for Greenland bore away

Bold Stevens was our captain's name
Our ship called the Lion so bold
And our poor souls our anchor away

  To face the storms and cold, brave boys
  To face the storms and cold

Oh when we arrived in that cold country
Our goodly ship to moor
We wished ourselves safe back again

  With those pretty girls on shore, brave boys
  With those pretty girls on shore

Our boatswain to the main top stand
With a spyglass in his hand
A whale a whale my lads he cries

  And she spouts at every span, brave boys
  And she spouts at every span

The captain walked the quarter-deck
And a jolly little fellow was he
Over haul over haul your davit tackle fall

    And we'll launch our boats all three brave boys
    And we'll launch our boats all three

There was harpineery and picaneery
And boat steerery also
And twelve jolly tars to tug at the oars

    And a-whaling we all go, brave boys
    And a-whaling we all go

We struck that whale and down she went
By the flourish of her tail
By chance we lost a man overboard

    And we did not get that whale, brave boys
    And we did not get that whale

When this news to our captain came
It grieved his heart full sore
And for the loss of a 'prentice boy

    It was half mast colors all, brave boys
    It was half mast colors all

It's now cold months is a-coming on
No longer can we stay here
For the winds do blow and the whales do go

    And the daylight seldom does appear, brave boys
    And the daylight seldom does appear

TRADITIONAL – 1833

The Sea Ran High

Larry Kaplan sang *The Sea Ran High* [14] at the Mystic Seaport Festival in 2017. The rediscovery of the tune is interesting. While living on Martha's Vineyard, Gale Huntington was presented with a journal, which one of his students had uncovered in a landfill. Huntington credits that the song "comes from an entry in the journal of the vessel *Lotus*, of Salem dated 1833." [15]

Another reference to the song was found in the *Sailor's Magazine and Naval Journal, Volume 5* published in 1833 which reports that the song was written by a young sailor in 1833 but the title was *On the Loss of Schooner Mechanic, Captain Holland*. [16]

> The wind blew hard the sea ran high
> And fast the snow fell from the sky
> When a little bark on our shore was cast
> And all on board but was lost.
>
> The hardy captain oft before
> Had suffered wrecks and trials sore
> But still he dared the seas to brave
> And leave his home for a watery grave.
>
> The other men were stout and bold
> But to the wreck they could not hold
> The angry waves rolled over their heads
> And sunk them in the deep like lead.
>
> But one alone of all the crew
> Who was both young and feeble too
> Yes he though weak outlived the gale
> To tell to all the fatal tale.

TRADITIONAL – 1833

The Captain Calls All Hands

Gale Huntington culled a version of the song *The Captain Calls All Hands* [17] from an 1832 journal of the whale ship *Bengal* of Salem. Cecil Sharp collected and published another version of this song in England. Although the words are the same, the American and English versions probably use different melodies. [18] The lyrics were also found in an even earlier version called *A Song Concerning Love*, which was found in Stephen Cahoon's journal from the *Polly* out of Gloucester dating back to 1794. In his book, *Jolly Sailors Bold Ballads and Songs of the American Sailor*, Stuart Frank calls *The Captain Calls All Hands* a sailor's farewell song, noting, "It is interesting that the two (earliest) manifestations in whalemen's journals are virtually the only vestiges of the song that have been found in North America and both transcriptions are from adjacent ports, Salem and Gloucester, on the so-called North Shore of Boston." [19]

> The Captain calls all hands away tomorrow
> Leaving all our girls behind in grief and sorrow
> Dry up your brimming tears, and cease of weeping
> How happy we shall be at our next meeting.
>
> Why will you go abroad to fight with strangers
> When you can stay at home, free from all dangers?
> For I need you in my arms, I need you by me
> So stay at home with me, do not deny me.
>
> Farewell to parents dear, father and mother
> I am your only daughter, you have no other
> And when you think of me, how I am grieving
> You will know the lad I love ruined me by leaving.

Down on the ground she fell, like someone dying
Lying there and crying, There's no believing
There's no believing, none; not one's dear lover
Excepting two agree, and love each other.

TRADITIONAL – 1832

Sharply Its Breath The Vessel Feels

This fragment *Sharply Its Breath the Vessel Feels* is from the logbook of the ship *George* detailing a voyage from Salem, Massachusetts to Calcutta, India and back again. The *George* left Salem on August 1831 and returned April 1832. The log keeper was Charles D. Mugford and owner was Joseph Peabody. [20]

Sharply its breath the vessel feels,
Down on her groaning side she keels;
Another reef is taken in---
Loudly she dreadful thunder peals,
Old Ocean, echoes to she dives:

Beneath she blow-
She rises slow

As smart the helmsman luff him when
We think no more, but just like men,
But clearly to our duty move,
And leave the future knows of Love.

TRADITIONAL – 1838

Blow! Oh Blow!

Blow! Oh Blow! was recorded in the logbook of the Salem ship *Borneo* owned by George Z. Silsbee of Salem. The logbook #983 details a voyage from Salem to Sumatra from December 1842 to September 1843. [21] The *Borneo* was a 297-ton ship that was registered in Salem on December 2, 1831. In 1834, the *Borneo* was altered to a Barque and abandoned in the North Atlantic in 1854.

> Blow! Oh Blow! Auspicious lives,
> Onward! Onward! Urge our war.
> Every flaw our good ships seized
> Wafts us towards "Boston Boys"

TRADITIONAL – 1842

Merrily, Merrily!

This fragment *Merrily, Merrily* is from the same *Borneo* logbook #983. [22]

> Merrily, Merrily, goes the bark,
> Before the gale she's bound;
> So darts the dolphin from the sharks,
> Or the deer before the hounds.

TRADITIONAL – 1842

Sir Walter Scott wrote a similar verse:

> Merrily, Merrily, bounds the Bark,
> She bounds before the gale.
> The mountain breeze from Ben-na-darch,
> Is joyous in her sails.[23]

The Wandering Sailor

Nathaniel Silsbee of Salem, Massachusetts wrote *The Wandering Sailor*[24] in the logbook of the ship *Astrea* Log #11. The logbook details a voyage from China to Java beginning in January 1789 and ending in February 1789. The owner was Elias Hasket Derby of Salem and the shipmaster was James Magee. *The Wandering Sailor* can also be found in *The Princess of Montserrat: Strange Narrative of Adventure and Peril on Land and Sea.*

> The wandering sailor plows the main
> A competence in life to gain
> Undaunted braves the stormy seas
> To find at last content and ease
> In hopes when toil and danger's o'er
> To anchor on his native shore
>
> When winds blow hard and mountains roll
> And thunders shake from pole to pole
> Tho dreadful waves surrounding foam
> Still flattering fancy wafts him home
> In hopes when toil and danger's o'er
> To anchor on his native shore
>
> When round the bowl the jovial crew
> The early scenes of life renew
> Tho each his favorite fair will boast
> This is the universal toast
> May we with toil and dangers o'er
> Cast anchor on our native shore.

TRADITIONAL – 1789

The Faithful Sailor

The Faithful Sailor [25] was found in the logbook #11 of the *Astrea* on its voyage from China to Java from January 1789 to February 1789. Elias Hasket Derby (known to his friends as Hasket) owned the ship and employed young Nathaniel Silsbee as the log keeper,

his first responsibility at sea as a 14 year old. Over time, Silsbee learned all the duties and responsibilities of being on board a ship and grew into one of Salem's notable merchants during his career, which lasted into the 1850s. The well-known composer of sea songs, Edward Thompson wrote *The Faithful Sailor* in 1765. He originally called the song *The Sailor's Farewell*, which can also be found in the Isaiah Thomas Broadside Ballads Project. [26]

Nathaniel Silsbee: *Biographical Notes*, Salem Collection, Salem Public Library, title page missing, no publication information available, courtesy of the Salem Public Library

The Faithful Sailor

The topsails shiver in the wind,
The ship she calls to sea,
But yet may soul, my heart sad minds,
Are Mary moor'd with thee,
For though my sailor's bound afar,
Still love shall be his leading star.

Should landsmen flatter when we're sail'd,
Oh doubt their artful tales!
No gallant sailor ever fails,
I have breath constant gales,
Thou art the comfort of my souls,
Which steers my heart from pale to pale.

Syrens in every port we find,
More fatal than rocks or waves,
But such as grace the British fleets,
Are lasses not slaves,
No fear can ever us subdue,
Although we leave our hearts with you.

There are the cases but if you so be kind,
We'll scorn on the dashing main,
The rocks, the billows, the wind,
'Till we return again,
New England's glory rests with you,
Our sails are full sweet girls, adieu.

EDWARD THOMPSON – 1765

~ 4 ~
Life at Sea

Home Again

Marshall S. Pike wrote the lyrics for *Home Again* [1] in 1850 and John P. Ordway of Salem composed the music. The music and song lyrics were found in the Broadside Collection, Center for Popular Music, Middle Tennessee State University. J. Peckman of 137 Essex Street, Salem, Massachusetts published the broadside Home Again, circa 1858.

>Home again, home again,
>From the foreign shore;
>And O, it fills my soul with joy,
>To meet my friends once more.
>Hear I drop the parting tear
>To cross the ocean's foam;
>But now I'm once again with those
>Who kindly greet me home.
>Home again, Home again.
>
>Happy hearts, happy hearts,
>With mine have laughed in glee:
>But O, the friends I loved in youth
>Seem happier to me,
>And if my guide should be my fate
>Which bids me longer roam
>But death alone can break the tie
>That binds my heart to home.
>Home again, Home again.
>
>Music sweet, music soft,
>Lingers round the place;
>And O, I feel the childhood charm,
>That time cannot offend

Life at Sea

Then give me but my homestead roof,
I'll ask no palace dome,
For I can live a happy life
Within those I love at home.
Home again, Home again.

MARSHALL S. PIKE AND JOHN P. ORDWAY – 1858

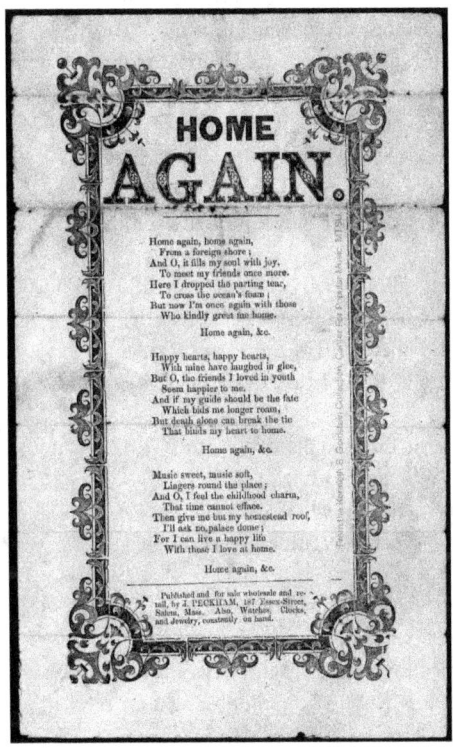

Home Again, courtesy of the Kenneth S. Goldstein Collection of American Song Broadsides, Center for Popular Music, Middle Tennessee State University

The Seaman

The Seaman[2] was transcribed from the *Salem Gazette* dated August 2, 1811.

While with fierce rage the wild winds roar,
And screaming frenzy's frantic foam
Loves mid the swelling din to pour
Loud dirges on the midnight storm;

Then vainly thinks the seaman bold,
While shivering with the rain and cold,
Oh! Had he sav'd his cash on shore,
He'd brave the faithless deep no more.

And calling to his cheerless mind,
How blest Landsman's he must be,
Who shelter'd from the rain and wind,
Laughs at the troubles of the sea-

Forms humble plans of future
A small seat cottage-and a
Resolv'd to save his cash on
And trust the faithless deep no

But soon the howling blast is
And peace resumes her tranquil
Fair blows the gale-the welcome shore,
He greets with longing eyes again,

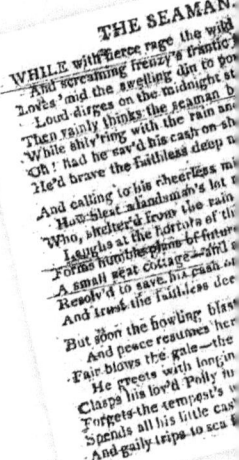

Life at Sea

Clasps his love Polly in his arms,
Forgets the tempest's wild alarms,
Spends all his little cash on shore,
And gaily trips to sea for more.

TRADITIONAL – 1811

The Sailor's Watch At Sea

The Sailor's Watch At Sea [3] was found in the *Salem Gazette* dated January 25, 1820.

Sleep, Sailor Sleep; and take thy rest;
    Sleep, Sailor sleep, and banish care,
For well thou knowest thy house is blest;
    And guarded by a fond wife's prayer.

Sleep, Sailor sleep; the storm is o'er,
    See younder! See the morning star,
And numerous blessings are in store
    Thy day of bliss is not afar.

The storms of life may o'er the blow
    And harmless burst beneath thy fest,
Activity may round the flow,
    And yet, thy blessings he complete:

Thy watch on deck, and watch below,
    Are emblems of life's changeful state,
The new and then his smiles we know
    Tho linked in bonds of the hardest fate.

TRADITIONAL – 1820

A Sailor's Life

A Sailor's Life [4] was culled the *Salem Gazette* circa 1810 and also found in William McCarty's *Songs, Odes, and Other Poems, on National Subjects: Part Two.*

HOW bless'd the life a sailor leads,
    From clime to clime still ranging,
For as the calm the storm succeeds,
    The scene delights by changing.
Though tempests howl along the main,
    Some object will remind us,
And cheer with hope to meet again,
    The friends we left behind us.

Then, under full sail, we laugh at the gale,
    Though the landsmen look pale, never heed 'em;
But toss off the glass to a favourite lass,
    To America, Commerce, and Freedom.

But when arrived in sight of land,
    Or safe in port rejoicing;
Our ship we moor, our sails we hand,
    Whilst out the boat is hoisting.
With cheerful hearts the shore we reach,
    Our friends delight to greet us;
And, tripping lightly o'er the beach,
    The pretty lasses meet us.

When the full-flowing bowl enlivens the soul,
    To foot it we merrily lead 'em;
And each bonny lass will drink off a glass
    To America, Commerce, and Freedom.

Our prizes sold, the chink we share,
    And gladly we receive it;
And when we meet a brother tar,
    That wants, we freely give it.
No freeborn sailor yet had store,
    But cheerfully would lend it;
And when 'tis gone, to sea for more;
    We earn it but to spend it.

Then drink round, my boys, 'tis the first of our joys
    To relieve the distress'd, clothe and feed 'em;
'Tis a duty we share with the brave and the fair,
    In this land of Commerce and Freedom.

TRADITIONAL – PRE 1842

A Sailor Boy

A Sailor Boy [5] was found in the *Salem Gazette* dated October 29, 1805.

Dark flew the scud along the wave,
And echoing thunders rend the sky;
All hands aloft! to meet the storm,
At midnight was the boatswain's cry.

On deck flew every gallant tar,
But one—bereft of ev'ry joy;
Within a hammock's narrow bound,
Lay stretch'd this hapless SAILOR BOY.

Once, when the Boatswain pip'd all hands,
  The first was he, of all the crew,
On deck to spring—to trim the sail—
  steer—to reef—to furl or clue.

Now fell disease had seiz'd a form
  nature cast in finest mould;
The midwatch bell now smote his heart,
  His last, his dying knell it toll'd.

"O God!" he cried, and gasp'd for breath,
  "Ere yet my soul shall cleave the skies,
"Are there no parents—brethren—near,
  "To close, in death, my weary eyes?

"All hands aloft to brave the storm,
  "I hear the wintry tempest roar;"
He rais'd his head to view the scene,
  And backward fell, to rise no more.

The morning sun in splendour rose.
The gale was hush'd and still'd the wave;
  The Sea-boy, far from all his friends,
  Was plung'd into a wat'ry grave.

But He, who guards the Sea-boy's head,
  He, who can save or can destroy,
Snatch'd up to Heav'n the purest soul
  That e'er adorn'd a SAILOR BOY.

TRADITIONAL – 1805

Life at Sea

A Sea Song

A Sea Song [6] was taken from the *Salem Gazette* dated January 19, 1798.

All hands on board, quick to the wind-lass haste;
Leave lustily, my breast! The anchor we'll weigh;

Heave O! now it comes Heave O! there avast!
She forestay sail loose – four able belay.

Low wind ship, my boys! She'll work like a top;
Farewell, ye dear girls! No longer we stop.

See the gentle breeze our bellying sails
Expand their white canvas, and flip by the shore;

Her sky looks serene, and propitious the gales;
Let no danger we fear, should the foul tempest roar;

Our homes just discerning, we bid them adieu;
Sweet girl, be ye mindful our hearts are with you.

Adieu then the shore, where all can enjoy
She scenes that gay frolic forever does give:

But the sailor who roves, him no terror annoy,
While the love-pouting lass bids affection to live;

Then cheerful he ransacks the world's mighty coast,
And where e'er he stops, loves and friendship's his toast.

TRADITIONAL – 1798

Heaving the Anchor

Heaving the Anchor [7] was uncovered in the *Salem Gazette* dated August 18, 1792.

When shifts hear the boatswain bray,
    With the voice like thunder roaring,
All hands, my lads, get under way;
    Hark, the signal for unmooring.
        To save the joyous breeze,
        Our handspikes quick to freeze
        In hopes to meet the foe-
Our capstan here, the windless there,
We man to the tune of heo, hea, heo, & c.

Cass loose tour topsails, next he cries,
    Top gallant-sails and courses
Clew line and gear, let go my boys,
    Haul home your sheets like horses,
        The mizzen too, be glib,
        Fore-staysail too, and gib,
        Your downhauls, boys, lets go;

We strait comply, and eager fly,
And obey to the tune of heo, hea, heo, & c.

The anchor's up, oh! Next they call,
    Avast boys 'vail your heaving,
Our cat and sills we overhaul,
    Our handspikes nimbly leaving;
        Then if a prosperous gale,
        We crowd on ev'ry fail,
        Our sheets they sweetly flow,

Life at Sea

Along we swim, our braces trim,
And it's all to the tune of heo, hea, heo, & c.

Then lovely Moll, and Sue, and Beck,
    Their eyes with grief o'er flowing,
With heavy hearts come up on deck,
    The rude winds on them blowing;
        A sport embrace we take,
        Which makes our hearts to ache,
        A while we're loft in woe;
Nor to our grief, can find relief,
Till cheer'd by the tune of heo, hea, heo, & c.

TRADITIONAL – 1792

The Anchor at Cabot Farm,
Salem, Massachusetts

The Fisherman's Orphan

The Fisherman's Orphan [8] was found in the *Salem Gazette* dated August 2, 1816.

An Orphan I am fearcely turned of twelve years
And Mary a begging I must go;
My father a fisherman, void of all fears,
On the wild billows tossed to and fro.

One night, all alone, as he brav'd the rough ocean,
The raging winds a blew in a dreadful commotion;
The boat was his coffin, the water his grave,
And low he lies buried beneath the green wave.

My mother, heart broken, to heaven is gone,
And left her poor Mary behind.
And now through the wide world I wander foreign,
To be of the good and the kind,

Though thinly I'm clad, with cold I now shiver,
Yet warm is my heart, and will bless the dear giver;
No friend has poor Mary from hunger to save,
Her father and mother lie low in the grave.

The sky is covering, the cold earth my bed,
When I lie down to slumber or weep:
And on the pale primrose I pillow my head,
While the winds sweetly lilt me to sleep.

Life at Sea

Then I see, in my dreams, my dear father returning,
And mix with sad fights the cold dew, of the morning;
But alas! Who could ever return from the grave;
And low he lies buried beneath the cold wave.

O, were I but rich, what a tomb I would rear,
To parents so tender and good;
O'er my mother's low hillock shed many a tear-
But my father lies deep in the flood.

The wild birds of ocean, as through the air sailing,
At midnight are heard o'er him mournfully wailing,
And gold gleaming sits beneath the green wave
With seaweed and coral shall deck his cold grave.

TRADITIONAL – 1816

Written at Sea in a Heavy Gale

Written at Sea in a Heavy Gale[9] was found in the *Salem Mercury* dated February 10, 1789.

Happy the man who's safe on shore
Now trim at home, his evening fire
Unmoved, he bears the tempest roars,
That on the tufted grove expire,

> Alas! On us they doubly fall,
> Our feeble barque must bear them all.

Now to the bounty the birds retreat,
The squirrels seeks, his hollow tree,
Wolves in their shaded caverns meet,
All, all are blest but wretched we;

> Freedom'd a stranger to repose,
> No rest th' unsettled ocean knows.

While o'ver the dark abyss we roam,
Perhaps whare're the pilots say,
We saw the fun, descent in gloom,
No more to see his rising ray;

> But bury'd lone, by far too deep,
> On coral beds, unpitied sleep!

But what a strange, uncoasted strand
Is that, where death permits no day;
No charts have we to mark that land,
No compass to direct the way,

Life at Sea

      What pilot shall explore the realm,
      What new Columbus takes the helm.

While death and darkness both surrounds,
And tempest rage with lawless power,
Of friendship's voice I hear no sound,
No comfort in this dreadful hour.

      What friendships can in tempest be,
      What comfort on this angry sea.

The barque, accustom'd to obey,
No more the trembling pilots guide,
Along she gropes her trackless way,
While mountains burst on either side:

      Thus, skill and science both must fall,
      And ruin is the lost of all.

TRADITIONAL – 1789

The Honest Sailor

The Honest Sailor [10] or *The Sailor* was culled from the October 1805 edition of the *Salem Gazette*. Charles Dibdin, from Britain, was a prolific singer-songwriter specializing in sea songs. He wrote and titled this song *The Girl Who'd Choose A Sailor*. Even though Dibdin had no connection to Salem, Dibdin's songs and poems were continuously published in the *Salem Gazette*. The songs appeared without any reference to the author and, on several occasions, the titles were altered. One thought is that the Gazette found his songs of interest to the people of Salem because of their close connection to the sea.

>The girl, who sain would choose a mate.
>>Should ne'er in fondness tail her,
>
>May thank her lucky stars, if fate,
>>Should splice her to a sailor;
>
>He braves the storm, the battle's heat,
>>The yellow boys to nail her;
>
>Diamonds, if diamonds the could eat
>>Would seek her honest sailor.

>If she'd be constant, still his heart
>>She's sure will never fail her;
>
>For though a thousand leagues apart,
>>Still faithful is her sailor;
>
>If she be false, still he is hence,
>>And absent does bewail her;
>
>Her trusting, as he trusts the wind,
>>Still faithless to the sailor.

Life at Sea

A butcher can provide her prog,
    Three threads to drink a tailor,
What's that to biscuit and to grog
    Procur'd her by her sailor?
She, who would such a mate refuse,
    The devil sure must ail her;
Search around, and, if you're wife, you'll choose
    To wed an honest sailor.

CHARLES DIBDIN – 1805

The Honest Sailor.

THE girl, who fain would chuſe a mate,
    Should ne'er in fondneſs tail her,
May thank her lucky ſtars, if fate
    Should ſplice her to a tailor:
He braves the ſtorm, the battle's heat,
    The yellow boys to nail her ;
Diamonds, if diamonds ſhe could eat,
    Would ſeek her honeſt Sailor.

If ſhe'd be conſtant, ſtill his heart
    She's ſure will never fail her ;
For though a thouſand leagues apart,
    Still faithful is her Sailor ;
If ſhe be falſe, ſtill he is hence,
    And abſent does bewail her ;
Her truſting, as he truſts the wind,
    Still faithleſs to the Sailor.

A butcher can provide her prog,
    Three threads to drink a tailor,
What's that to biſcuit and to grog
    Procur'd her by her Sailor?
She, who would ſuch a mate refuſe,
    The Devil ſure muſt ail her ;
Search round, and, if you're wife, you'll chooſe
    To wed an honeſt Sailor.

The Honest Sailor, Salem Gazette, October 8, 1805, #1473

Harriet Low

Harriet Low (Hillard) was born in Salem in 1809. She was one of the first American women to sail to China with a trade expedition. She shipped aboard the *Sumatra*. Margaret Christman who wrote *Adventurous Pursuits* states that during her stay in China, she wrote a journal in the form of letters to her older sister Molly. While in China, Low's duty was to be a companion to her sickly aunt. Not being allowed on the mainland, Low tried to dress up as a man in order to pursue her interests but was discovered. She soon became acquainted with many of the well-known residents, including the painter George Chinnery. [11]

Daisy Nell is a local folk musician living in Essex, Massachusetts. She wrote the song *Harriet Low* in 1992. Daisy performs folk music with her husband Stan and has written six children's books including *The Stowaway Mouse* and *Rocky at The Dockside*.

Harriet Low, on a day long ago
On board the Sumatra set sail
A companion to Aunt, an adventure jaunt
In her diary recorded this tale.

On the day they set sail other boats did regale
And at Baker's they bid them adieu
At twenty years old to be gone from the fold
She hoped that her dreams would come true.

For her sister at home, all the places she'd roam
Were noted in flowery detail
To sail night and day, the ports on the way
In comparison Salem seemed pale.

Life at Sea

    And away from Salem's elegant home
    Across the ocean to China did roam
    To live in Macao while menfolk went on
    Up the Pearl River to trade at Canton.

An artist of fame, George Chinnery came
And in time he did teach her to draw
While Harriet learned, for excitement she yearned
But she had to adhere to the law.

Sweet Harriet tried, the ways to abide
Which kept women out of the Hong
But with Aunt she did dare and they tucked up their hair
And as sailors they made for Canton.

They did not deceive and were ordered to leave
Or an end to all commerce they'd see
They say curiously did in the cat
But it seemed it was her cup of tea.

    And away from Salem's elegant home
    Across the ocean to China did roam
    To live in Macao while menfolk went on
    Up the Pearl River to trade at Canton.

Now she looks at us all from her frame on the wall
Dressed in her glamorous clothes
Now behold her sweet blush by George Chinnery's brush
As she smiles in her innocent pose.

    And away from Salem's elegant home
    Across the ocean to China did roam
    To live in Macao while menfolk went on
    Up the Pearl River to trade at Canton.

DAISY NELL – 1992

Again to Mary Dear

Again to Mary Dear [12] was written in the logbook of the *Bark Sea Mew* out of Salem. The log keeper was William Smith The logbook details a voyage from Salem to the Kingdom of Loango beginning March 1849 and ending November 1849. The owners of the *Sea Mew* were Robert Brookhouse and William Hunt.

> Shake haste ye hours fly swiftly away,
>   Let me no longer mourn;
> I long to see that happy day,
>   When Johnny will return.
>
> Oh! Johnny dear return once more,
>   To bless thy Mary true;
> Then I again will hear no more,
>   The parting word adieu.
>
> Oh dearest, don't think of me,
>   While on the foaming main;
> Shall those kinds words that fell from thee,
>   To Mary e'er prove vain.
>
> Oh no! For thou wilt ever prove,
>   My kindest, dearest friend;
> Where pure and never dying love,
>   For one, shall have no ends.
>
> A sailor's love I'm often told,
>   Soon fades like evening skies,
> Or like a flower, twill soon grow old,
>   And like the flower it dies.
>
> But I will trust my Johnny's heart,
>   Neath any .... Or sun;
> Tho boundless oceans may us part,
>   We'll e'er be true to once.

> Then blow! Oh Blow! Ye fair winds blow,
> And bear my treasure here;
> The greatest wealth I e'er can know,
> Again to Mary dear.

TRADITIONAL – 1849

The Seaman's Home

The Seaman's Home [13] was found in the *Salem Gazette* dated July 22, 1803. This song reflects the difficulty of life at sea and the fear that Salemites endured as sailors went to sea. It is also called *O You Whose Lives*, which was found in *The Vocal Library, a collection of English, Scottish and Irish Songs*. [13]

The Seaman's Home, Salem Gazette, July 22, 1803, #1242

Oh ye, whose lives on land are pass'd,
And keep from dang'rous seas aloof,
Who careless listen to the blast,
Or beating rains upon the roof;
You little heed how seamen fare,
Condemn'd the angry storm to bear.

Sometimes when breakers vex the tide,
He takes his station on the deck;
And now lash'd over the vessel's side,
He clears away the cumb'ring wreck-
And while the billow o'er him foam,
The Ocean is his only home.

Still fresher blows the midnight gale,
"All hands reef top-sails," are the cries,
And while the clouds the heaven's veil,
Aloft to reef the sail he flies!
In storms so rending, doom'd to roam,
The ocean is the seamen's home.

TRADITIONAL – 1803

Come All Good People

    Log keeper Edward Beacham on October 18, 1774 wrote down the ballad *Come All Good People* [14] in logbook # 3 of the *Eagle*. *The Eagle* was a whaling schooner out of the North Shore of Massachusetts. There is no indication of who composed the ballad or whether the event described actually occurred but, nevertheless, it is an interesting story line. A terrible storm arose, many men were lost at sea and a few men survived and were rescued to tell their story.

Come all good people young and old I will unto tell
It's of a malloneoly thing that lately hear befell.
It was two vessels lately saild & was for Ginea Bouno
A whaling voige was their intent to cruse the ocean round.

Before the wind & sea did saild which canvas did supply
But little though on souls on bord that danger was so nigh,
Till on a mighty shold they struck where billows loud did rore
It Stove their boats in pieces small & overbord did por.

The schooner was the first that struck her mast, she quickly lost
But sum small sparse that they did save with which the sholes they crost
The slope her quarter deck came of Gods goodness to fulfill
One which 1 day 2 nights they tosst the ellements was still.

O call and see & turn you round upon the Noble Plain
And see how gracious god has been unto the race of Man
He bids the furious clouds stan still & they obey his voice
Had they the ellements at will they could have no better choice.

Life at Sea

When on this Shole they first did strick the winds it was but finale
But suddenly it Shifted Round & what was worst than all,
The tide against the wind did strive which made the bellows to rore
But heave they struck upon this Shold feel five leags from the shore.

The loking round with akeing hearts thought every man must die
For then they struck upon this shold & raced most dismally
O think you mortals great & small how mortal man must feal,
To hear the sounds of bitters cries when they lay on the heal.

But won thing more I have to tell this heavy News come home
For Capt Squirse one boat he sent who told the rest was gone,
Then people mustred far & near A listing hands to lend
A vessel in their sight Did Soon appear which quickly they did send

But they did soon return again with heavy News to tell
No sight Nor sound of Any thing which made Sum hearts to swell
Som for their husbands Loud Did Cry Some for their children Dear
To things that they all Drowned was & Nothing more could hear.

But he that conkers Deth & hell their gardia angel bore
In his right hand he held the wind & brought them to the Shore

EDWARD BEACHAM – 1774

Fair Salem Town

Fair Salem Town or *A Seaman and His Love* [15] was found in the Helen Hartness Flanders ballad collection at Middlebury College in Vermont. The song was collected for the Flanders's collection by Marguerite Onley and recorded on audiocassette on April 22, 1942, and sung by Belle Luther Richards of Colebrook, New Hampshire. Richards stated in the notes that she "learned from her father, Luther of Pittsburgh, New Hampshire, who was born in Canada." [15]

Portrait of a young Helen Hartness Flanders published in the *Salem Evening News* [16] date unknown. Used with permission from Helen Hartness Ballad Collection, Middlebury College

This song, also known as *A Seaman and His Love* is from a family of sailor songs referred to as the Riley Ballads or Broken Token Ballads. Just before the sailor goes off to sea, he gives his lover one half of a token saying he will be back to marry her. When he returns, he dresses in a disguise to see if she has been truthful about waiting for him to return. When she resists his tricks, he surprises her with his half of the token and takes off his disguise to her great delight as she welcomes him home.

Since versions of this song were sung on both sides of the Atlantic, words could be changed depending on the port. Possibly a sailor from Salem changed the name to *Fair Salem Town*.

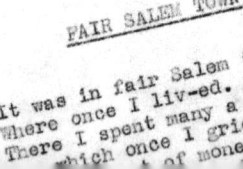

Life at Sea

Fair Salem Town

I was in Fair Salem Town, Where once I liv-ed.
There I spent many a crown, For which once I griev-ed.
For the want of money in store, I was forced to wander
This wide world o'er and o'er; Yet I feared no danger.

It was on one November night, Being dark all over;
The moon it gave no light, That you could discover.
Down by the water side, Where fine ships were sailing,
I spied a pretty fair maid, Weeping and wailing.

I stepped up to her; Said I, "My dear, what grieves you?"
She made me a reply; "you cannot relieve me.
They have pressed my love, " she cried, "To plow the ocean;
My heart is like the sea, always in motion."

And these were his last works, "Oh, take a token
Unto the girl I love; None could love fairer.
Unto the girl I love; None could love fairer;
And tell her to prove kind, and wed the bearer.

It was when she heard these words, She grew quite distracted.
She knew not what she done, or how she acted.
"Young man, you are too late; You are a ranger;
Young man, you are too late; I'll wed no stranger."

Then seeing her love so strong, made mind the stranger.
I threw off my disguise; I could wait no longer.
She said, "You are my love, my own true lover,
And by all else above, I'll wed no other."

....
....

Where we sat down to sing, and she sang more clearer,
Than a nightingale in spring; "Welcome home, my lover."

TRADITIONAL – UNKNOWN

Sweet William and Gentle Jenny

The ballad *Sweet William and Gentle Jenny* was found in *George Nichols; Salem Ship Master and Merchant: An Autobiography* [17] as a recitation performed by his daughter Miss Lydia Ropes Nichols of Salem, Massachusetts. George Nichols was a famous captain of the ship *Active*, out of Salem. Mary Augusta Scott wrote in *The Magazine of History with Notes and Queries*, one "summer a lady sang to me a *Ballad of Sweet William* as quaint in tune as it is quaint in words. She told me that she had learned the ballad from her aunt (Miss Lydia Ropes Nichols) who in turn had learned it from her father (George Nichols)." [18] Scott continued on saying that when his ship was becalmed, and the men were depressed, Nichols would ask one of the sailors from Down East to sing *Sweet William* which always seemed to cheer the crew. [18]

Francis Child wrote in his book *English and Scottish Popular Ballads* that the ballad #277 *The Wife Wrapped in Wether's Skin* variant F has an American version called *Sweet William and Gentle Jenny*. He also references Miss Lydia R. Nichols of Salem, Massachusetts as the source of the ballad. [19]

> Sweet William he married a wife,
>   Gentle Jenny cried Rosemaree,
> To be the sweet comfort of his life,
>   As the dew flies over the mulberry tree.
>
> Jenny couldn't in the kitchen to go,
>   Gentle Jenny cried Rosemaree,
> For fear of dirtying her white-heeled shoes,
>   As the dew flies over the mulberry tree.

Jenny couldn't wash, and Jenny couldn't bake,
    Gentle Jenny cried Rosemaree,
For fear of dirtying her white apurn tape,
    As the dew flies over the mulberry tree.

Jenny couldn't card, and Jenny couldn't spin,
    Gentle Jenny cried Rosemaree,
For fear of hurting her gay gold ring,
    As the dew flies over the mulberry tree.

Sweet William came whistling in from plaow,
    Gentle Jenny cried Rosemaree,
Says, "O my dear wife, is my dinner ready naow,"
    As the dew flies over the mulberry tree.

She called him a dirty paltry whelp,
    Gentle Jenny cried Rosemaree,
"If you want any dinner, go get it yourself,"
    As the dew flies over the mulberry tree.

Sweet William went aout unto the sheep-fold,
    Gentle Jenny cried Rosemaree,
And about a fat whether he did pull,
    As the dew flies over the mulberry tree.

And daown on his knees he began for to stick,
    Gentle Jenny cried Rosemaree,
And quicklie its skin he thereof did strip,
    As the dew flies over the mulberry tree.

He took the skin and laid on his wife's back,
    Gentle Jenny cried Rosemaree,
And with a good stick went whikety whack,
    As the dew flies over the mulberry tree.

I'll tell my father and all my kin,"
    Gentle Jenny cried Rosemaree,
"How still a quarrel you've begun,"
    As the dew flies over the mulberry tree.

"You may tell your father and all your kin,
    Gentle Jenny cried Rosemaree,
How I have thrashed my fat wether's skin,"
    As the dew flies over the mulberry tree.

Sweet William came whistling in from plaow,
    Gentle Jenny cried Rosemaree,
Says, " Oh my dear wife, is my dinner ready naow?"
    As the dew flies over the mulberry tree.

She drew her table and spread her board,
    Gentle Jenny cried Rosemaree,
And, "Oh my dear husband," was every word,
    As the dew flies over the mulberry tree.

And naow they live free from all care and strife,
    Gentle Jenny cried Rosemaree,
And naow she makes William a very good wife,
    As the dew flies over the mulberry tree.

TRADITIONAL – 1800s

The Disconsolate Sailor

Joseph Valpey, Jr. wrote *The Disconsolate Sailor* [20] in his prison log book while at Dartmore (sic) Prison.

    When my money was all gone that I gained in the wars
        And the world began to frown on my fate

Life at Sea

What matter'd my Zeal or my honoured Scar's
When indifference stood at each Gate.

The face that would smile when my purse was well lined
Shew'd a different aspect to Me
And when that I could nought but Ingratitude find
I hi 'd once again to the Sea.

I thought it unwise to repine at my Lot
Or to bare the Cold looks on the Shore
So I pack'd up the trifling remains I'd got
And a trifling alas was my store.

A handkerchief held all the treasures I had
Which over my shoulder I threw
Away then I trudg'd with a heart rather sad
To Join some Jolly Ship's Crew

The Sea was less troubled by far then my mind
For when the wide main I survey'd
I could not helping the world was unkind
And fortune a slippery jade.

And I vowed if once more I could take her in tow
I'd let the ungreatful one see
That the turbulent winds and the billows could show
More kindness than they did to me.

JOSEPH VALPEY, JR. – 1814

Living in a Seaport Town

Gerry Ryan wrote *Living in a Seaport Town* [21] in 2011 and the song was recorded on his CD *Today and Yesteryear*. Ryan, a long-time Salem resident, wrote this song while living in Salem referencing the romantic notions of New England, sailing, the ocean smells, and his ocean-side community of friends and loved ones. Ryan a local folk musician still calls Salem his home.

The harbor's cold and dark and grey,
Here on this fine September day,
As I slowly make my way,
Out to my boat at the head of the bay.

I always knew it dwelt in me,
Internal longing for the sea,
An echo calling for the coast,
It was a life I wanted the most.

    Chorus: Living in a seaport town,
             Tide comes in, tide goes down,
             I marvel at the life I found,
             When you're living in a seaport town.

The smell of the brisk, salty sea air,
The boat in the harbor waiting there,
For their Captains to arrive,
Raise up their sails and become alive.

And I have found the finest friends,
On whom my sanity depends,
They are hard working, loyal and true,
They are the ones who I raise my glass to.

Life at Sea

    Chorus: Living in a seaport town,
               Tide comes in, tide goes down,
               I marvel at the friends I found,
               When you're living in a seaport town.

This seaport town, it is my home,
New England brick and wood and stone,
The wild Atlantic rolling on,
Lifting my heart from the dust till the dawn.

I could not ask much more of life,
Somehow I found the perfect wife,
Love astounds in many ways,
He'll remain till the end of our days.

    Chorus: Living in a seaport town,
               Tide comes in, tide goes down,
               I marvel at the love I found,
               When you're living in a seaport town.

                                            Gerry Ryan – 2011

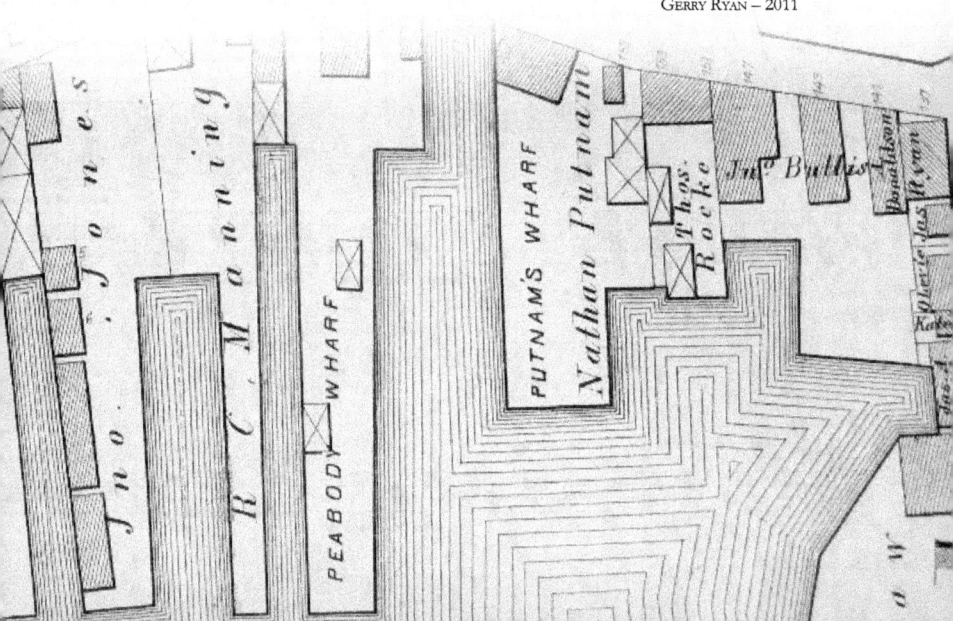

Salem Artillery

~ 5 ~
Death at Sea

On The Death of A Tar

The song *On The Death of a Tar* [1] was found in the *Salem Gazette* dated July 1807. The song goes by two other names: *Death of Frank Fid*, listed in the Country Dance & Song Society dated 1803, and a version called *Captain Glen's Unhappy Voyage to New-Barbary*. One of the survivors of the *Apollo* shipwreck wrote a narrative called the *Loss of His Majesty's Frigate Apollo* in 1804 in which the song was included using the *Death of Frank Fid* title.[2]

Frank Fid was a tar d'ye see,
    As true as e'er handled the sail,
Though the ship's gunnel in, yet still he
    Would laugh at the noise of the gale.
With his grog 'gainst the storm he prepared
    And squirted the juice of the quid;
Now below, now toss'd high on the yard,
    Twas all just the same to Frank Fid.

One day, off the Cape of Good Hope,
    As head to the wind lying to,
His foot took the bite of the rope,
    And Blud'd poor Frank's skull on the fluke,
The Doctor was sounding his brain,
    While the blood from is scuppers ran fast;
"Avast!" (he cried) caulking's in vain,
    For Death has sheer-hulk'd me at last.

On The Death of a Tar, Salem Gazette,
July 17, 1807, #1659, #93, vol. II

Death at Sea

"Come, messmates, no longer deplore;
      What's life! But a squall, at the best;
And tho'f I can cheer you no more,
      I mount in the truck of the blest;
I never fear'd danger nor toil,
      While an inch of life's brace stood the shock,
But now the last flake of my coil,
      Is recev'd through eternity's block.

Through life's stormy sea as I sail'd,
      By the compass of Friendship I steer'd,
And ne'er by Distress was I had'd
      But my lockers still open appear'd;
And whilst with a shot they would be stor'd
      None ever unaided went by,
When grog they no more would afford,
      I gave all I had-'twas a sigh.

I feel I must weigh-while I speak
      Death's capstan heaves short on my heart-
My anchor is almost a peak-
      What then? I have acted my part;
Safe birth'd in Felicity's bay,
      I shall ride by the kedge of Delight!
Gi's your hands then-no more he could say,
      His soul went aloft in our sight.

TRADITIONAL – 1804

The Dying Sailor Boy

The Dying Sailor Boy [3] was culled from a *Salem Gazette* published in 1811. A version of the poem was also found in *The Log Book; Or Nautical Miscellany, By Old Sailor,* published in 1930.

> Dark flew the scud along the wave,
> Repeated thunders rolled on high;
> All hands aloft the storm to brave,
> At midnight was the boatswain's cry.
>
> On deck sprang every soul apace;
> But one, bereft of human joy,
> Within a hammock's narrow space
> Lay stretched — a hapless sailor boy.
>
> Once when the boatswain's pipe would hail,
> The first was he of all the crew
> On deck to spring, to trim the sail,
> To steer, to reef, to furl or clew.
>
> Now fell disease had seized a form,
> Which Nature cast in happiest mold;
> The bell struck midnight through the storm,
> His last, his funeral knell it told.
>
> "Oh! God," he cried, and dropped a tear,
> "Before my spirit mounts the skies,
> Are there no friends, or messmates dear,
> To close in death my weary eyes?"

All hands aloft, loud blows the wind,
Surrounding billows loudly roar;
He raised his head, he bowed resigned,
Then backward sank to rise no more.

The morning sun in splendor rose,
The gale was hush'd, and still'd the wave;
The sea-boy found his last repose,
In ocean's deep and boundless grave.

But He who guards the sea-boy's head,
He who can save, or can destroy,
Caught the pure spirit as it fled,
And raised to heaven the sailor boy.

TRADITIONAL – 1811

Bury Me, Bury Me, Quick, Quick

Adoriram Judson was born in Malden, Massachusetts on August 9, 1788 and attended Brown University before enrolling as a student in Andover Seminary. Judson, the first American missionary, was ordained and commissioned at the Tabernacle Church in Salem on February 6, 1812 and left Salem Harbor on the ship *Caravan* for Burma to spread the gospel to "foreign lands." [4] On April 12, 1850, after many years as a missionary, he passed away aboard the ship *Aristide* on his way to the Isle of France and was buried at sea. Phineas Stowe, a preacher to seamen, wrote the following in his book titled *Ocean Melodies*, "Almost the last words of this great and good man, were 'Bury me, bury me, quick, quick,' and his voice failed." [5]

Phineas Stowe supplied the expression, "In the sea" to this moving request of the dying Christian. As Stowe says, "It may, or it may not have been his wish to be buried in the deep. His wide grave however, is emblematical of the vast moral influence he has had in arousing a slumbering world to the subject of foreign missions, in which sublime cause he had devoted over thirty years of untiring toil to promote. He expressed his views freely of the vast importance of converted mariners in the work of evangelizing the world. He was a friend to seaman, and they with others, performed the last sad office of committing his cold remains to the bosom of the 'great and wide sea.' His last words suggested the lines dedicated to his memory." [5]

Bury Me, Bury Me, Quick, Quick

Bury me, bury me, quick, quick – in the sea!
Thy grave will be far from the "Hopia Tree,"
And far from the "Rock" where the lov'd is at rest,
The ocean beneath her, turf on her breast.

Death at Sea

Bury me, bury me, quick, quick – in the sea!
It's the emblem of One who died on the Tree. –
Thy grave it is boundless, and pure like his throne,
And o'ver it he mirrors the works he hath done.

Bury me, bury me, quick, quick – in the sea!
What tomb could be chosen more fitted for
Thou loved the bright sea and over it had sailed,
To the land where gross darkness long had prevailed.

Bury me, bury me, quick, quick – in the sea!
From toil and from sorrow the lov'd one is free;
Thy anchor is cast in the sea of God's love;
Thy soul on bright pinions is carried above.

Yes! They buried thee quick, in the cold, blue deep,
At the calm hour of eve, when the winds were asleep,
Around thee were gathered the true and the brave,
And tears of affection were shed over thy grave.

The waves that roll over the noble one's form;
The calm breath of summer, and the loud howling storm,
Over the Jewel we've lost, their requiem sung;
Will waft the sad sound to each kindred and tongue.

PHINEAS STOWE – 1858

Bury Me, Bury Me, Quick, Quick Part II

The champion has fallen! Life's battle is over,
He's landed above on the Victor's bright shore;
Where death cannot enter, no foe can affright,
In that "mansion prepared," all, all is delight.

Sublime was thy life,- and the wide ocean grave,
Both blending in one, to embalm and engrave
Deep, deep on the heart, thy works in dark climes,
Where the Lamp Of Salvation brightly now shines.

The word of Immanuel by thee spread abroad,
Will gladded the gloomy with smiles from the Lord;
Yes! Millions shall bow to the might of that power,
That cheered thy rapt soul in death's trying hour.

In the deep, dark ocean thy body shall rest;
Till the archangel's trump shall sound its last blast;
Then, from thy wide tomb the body shall rise,
With myriads of "Burmese" ascend the bright skies.

How joyous the greeting, when lov'd ones shall meet
On the banks of deliverance, with melody sweet,
And chant all in union the Lamb's dying love,
In crowning, and saving, the ransomed above.

PHINEAS STOWE – 1858

Burn the Ships

The Tabernacle Church in Salem is known throughout the world because the first ever ordination and commissioning service for missionaries to foreign lands was held there on February 6, 1812. Dr. Samuel Worcester, the pastor at Tabernacle, was a leading force in the new missionary movement. With Salem's accessibility to the sea, it was natural and inevitable that the first such service should be held in Tabernacle Church. [6] To honor the landmark event, the settee upon which the new missionaries, Adoniram Judson, Samuel Newel, Samuel Nott, Gordon Hall and Luther Rice, were seated during the ceremony is preserved and on view in the Tabernacle Church's Historic Room.

The Historic Missionary Settee (1912 photo), courtesy of the Tabernacle Church's Historic Room

According to the *Essex Register's* article, *Ship News*, dated February 19, 1812, "the *Caravan* and *Heard* headed to Calcutta are cleared to leave the port of Salem." [7] *Burn the Ships* was written by Phineas Stowe and sung to the tune of *Bounding Billows*. Stowe states that, "Dr. Judson's constancy of purpose, which never flagged, nor sought retreat nor change, and in the consciousness of its indomitable strength, led him, on reaching the shores of Burma, (Myanmar) in his own significant language to 'Burn the Ships'." [8] Judson was now in Burma; he was committed to stay and begin his work with no retreat possible.

Burn the Ships

Burn the Ships, I'm safely landed,
In this clime of gloom and wo;
I would toil amid its darkness
And the seed of glory sow.

Burn the Ships, my heart is throbbing
To unfold Christ's banner here;
I would not return, but wander
O'er this land with tidings dear.

Burn the Ships, my soul is kindling
With a love that's firm on high,
To diffuse aboard a radiance,
Cheer the desolate who sigh.

Burn the Ships, I now am moored
In a dark and angry sea;
Yet above the sky is brilliant,
And bright Bethlehem's Star I see.

Burn the Ships, who would not toil
    In a field so full of thorns,
With his master's bow around me,
    What are life's tempestuous storms?

Burn the Ships, do not decoy me
    From the land I love so well;
Jesus died to save the heathen,
    I would his glad tidings tell.

Burn the Ships, I would remember
    His command to spread aboard
New of that redemption purchased
    By suffering, dying Lord.

Burn the Ships, the heathen calls me,
    I would listen to their moan;
Rapt they are in stable garments,
    Hark! They wall and sigh and groan.

Burn the Ships, I here must suffer
    In the prison night and day:
While the heathen's rage and fury
    Urge me on in heaven's highway.

Burn the Ships, here I would linger
    Till my Master calls me home;
Then with sheaves for him I've gathered
    Bow around his radiant throne.

PHINEAS STOWE – 1858

Melancholy Situation
*For the relations of the unfortunate people
left on the wreck of the Margaret*

Jonathan Plummer was a traveling preacher from Newbury who wrote a sermon and this song *Melancholy Situation* about the fatal shipwreck of *The Margaret*. According to the commander, Captain Fairchild, the ship had 46 persons on board for her passage from Naples to Salem. A horrific storm dismasted the ship but all passengers survived. When much of the rigging was cut away, the ship righted. "She was then so filled that little if any of her hull was left out of water." [9] Captain Fairchild and 14 others left the ship in a long boat and were rescued a few days later. The remaining 31 men and boys were left on board on May 21, 1810 with a "considerable supply of fresh water and good provisions" [9] but all perished.

Plummer wrote the ballad about the event to give comfort to others but he made a little money on the side by selling his broadside.

As on of Jesus sent to preach,
My dying friends I you beseech,
To give your hearts and souls to God,
And well regard his hand and rod.
Be ever willing he should reign,
And be the God of earth and main;
Be Christians meek and undefil'd
To him that made him reconcil'd.

He can preserve and can destroy,
He can give gifts, and can give joy,

He can poor ship-wreck'd men preserved,
Can feed them well, or can them starve,
Can send them quickly down to hell,
Or send them home his grave to tell:
And we should be good Christians mild,
To our dear Maker reconcil'd.

He can relieve their many woes,
And save them all from all their foes,
Can take them in consummate love,
To endless bliss in realms above,
And make them bless the solemn day,
That they are each a lovely child,
To God his father reconcil'd.

Yes, what he pleases he can do,
And all he does is holy too.
Then let us stop our poignant grief,
And trust in him for sweet relief,
Still pressing on by night and day,
In the good straight and narrow way,
That Satan may with grief be wild,
And we to God be reconcil'd.

Nor let us dare to scorn the Lord,
Or disregard his lovely word,
Less he should make his vengeance smoke,
And all the bones we've got be broke,
And our poor souls with fury hurl'd,
Should in an ever blazing world,
Forever mourn, that much beguil'd,
We ne'er to God were reconcil'd!

JONATHAN PLUMMER – 1810

Yankee Jack *A Song*

An early version of *Yankee Jack* [10] found in an 1808 *Salem Gazette* and titled *A Song*.

WHEN Jack was on the giddy mast,
    And lightning danced along the shrouds;
When every moment seem'd the last,
    And death frown'd threatening from the clouds;

Jack cast a tearful eye around,
And thought upon his native valley;
And mid the pealing thunder's sound,
His voice was heard, "Farewell, my Sally."

The storm soon ceased; the winds were hush'd,
    The mirth-inspiring can was quaff'd,
Jack for his former terrors blush'd,
    And at the recent danger laugh'd.

A soft emotion in his breast
Still brought to mind his native valley,
And ere his lips the bumper press'd,
He, smiling, toasted lovely Sally.

When war's red pennant raised on high
    Appear'd the signal for attack,
New courage beam'd from every eye,
    But not a soul more bold than Jack:

A Song, Salem Gazette, December 30, 1808

A fervent prayer to heaven he sigh'd
For blessings on his native valley;
"I care not for my fate," he cried,
"But if I fall, O bless my Sally."

His guardian angel heard the prayer,
    And wept that it was breathed so late;
For at that moment, from afar,
    Flew the shrill whistling ball of fate.

Jack wounded fell, and fainting cried,
"Farewell, my dear, my native valley,"
And as life's current ebb'd, he sigh'd,
"Farewell forever, lovely Sally."

TRADITIONAL – 1808

Blow on! Blow on! The Pirate's Glee

Blow On! Blow On! is also known as the *Storm at Sea in a Schooner*.[11] Considered a pirate ballad, the lyrics were written by Arthur Morrill in 1840. The music was composed by Benjamin F. Baker and respectfully dedicated to the Salem Glee Club. The text was found in Broadside Collection, at the Center for Popular Music, at Middle Tennessee State University. [12]

Blow on! Blow on! We love the howling
Of winds that waft us o'er the sea,
As fearless as the wolf that's prowling
Upon our native hills are we.

The doom'd in terror fly before us-
We've nailed the black flag to the mast;
It there shall float triumphant o'er us-
We will defend it to the last.

Roll on! Roll on! we love the motion
Of the waves that bear us on our way;
No swifter bark e'er sailed the ocean-
No skiff more lightly skims the bay.

The lightning from the sky is flashing –
The thunder's distant roar we hear;
But while o'er seas we thus are dashing,
We waves nor winds nor lightning's fear.

Flash on! Flash on! we love the gleaming,
That through the darkness shows our way;
The black flag is proudly streaming,
As proudly as it floats by day.

The waves roar with the thunder mingling,
Is music that we love to hear;
The lightning's flash at midnight shining,
Shows us a scene forever dear.

ARTHUR MORRILL – 1840

The Tale of the Sea

Found on the Library of Congress's website, *The Tale of the Sea* [13] was written by F. E. Weatherly and published in 1885 in Salem by the Salem Music Company.

Death at Sea

What is the tale of it, mother?
What is the tale of the wide, wide sea?
Merry and sad are the tales, my darling.
Merry and sad are the tales, must be.

Those ships that sail in the happy mornings,
Full of lives and the souls of men,…
Some will never come back my darling,
Some will never come back again.

Where are they gone, o mother?
Why is it cruel, the wide, wide, sea?
Tears and smiles are our lot, my darling,
Shadows and sun in the world must be,

They hear no longer the loud waves beating,
They feel… no longer the cold, cold foam,
They sleep as sweetly in the sea, my darling,
As you in your little bed at home.

Will it be so, forever, mother?
That friends must sever and tears must fall?
Not forever, my child, forever
This world is not the end of all.

All will be changed, the earth and ocean,
We know not how, and we know not when,
But those who have loved in this world, my darling,
Will meet in that world and be happy then.

F. E. WEATHERLY – 1885

The Tale of the Sea, courtesy of the Sheet Music
Division of the Library of Congress

Dame Alice Was Sitting on Widow's Walk

This Salem version of the Child Ballad # 85 *Lady Alice* is called *Dame Alice Was Sitting on Widow's Walk*. Thomas F. Leary of Durham, North Carolina contributed *Dame Alice Was Sitting on Widow's Walk* to *The Frank C. Brown Collection of North Carolina Folklore* in 1940. According to Leary, John McClusky of Salem, sang this song. "It is the story given a seaside setting. The widow's walk in New England seacoast towns is a place on the roof of the house where a woman could walk and watch for the return of ships that had gone out." [14] The woman hoping, wondering and praying that her husband would return from sea.

Salem Map, 1820, Author's Personal Collection

The Seamen's Widow and Orphan Association of Salem was formed May 1, 1833 and incorporated in March 1844. The original purpose of the organization was to give relief to the widows and orphans of seamen. [15]

In 1839, Children's Friend Society was officially formed and Reverend Michael Carlton of Tabernacle Church opened his home on Briggs Street to orphan children. In 1844, the group recieved

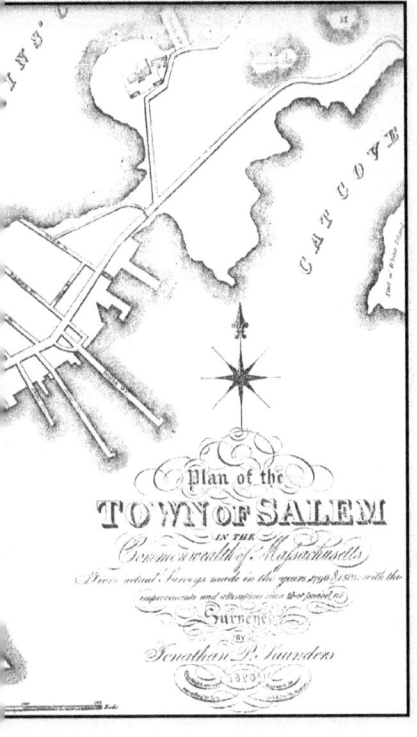

a bequest to open a home on Carpenter Street on the condition "Seaman's Orphan" be added to its name and it became "Seaman's Orphan and Children's Friend Society." [15]

In the early 20th century, the orphanage was closed. The agency, then named the Children's Friends and Family Service Society, became an adoption agency and a "friendly home visitor" agency, working to strengthen families. Over the last 20 years, the agency Children's Friend and Family Services has changed again in response to the needs of youth and families, developing counseling, mentoring, day care and juvenile court services, and becoming a county-wide organization, with offices in Lynn, Salem, Gloucester, Amesbury, and Lawrence. Its programs now serve over 5,000 youth and family members yearly. [15]

Not only were there services for widows and their children, Seamen's Bethels were scattered around Salem offering support and religion to old sailors. According to the *Salem Evening News* dated 1896, there were several Bethels with daily church services including the Hadley Rescue Mission in the Phoenix Building, The Marine Society Bethel at the foot of Turner Street and Seamen's Bethel on Derby Street. [16]

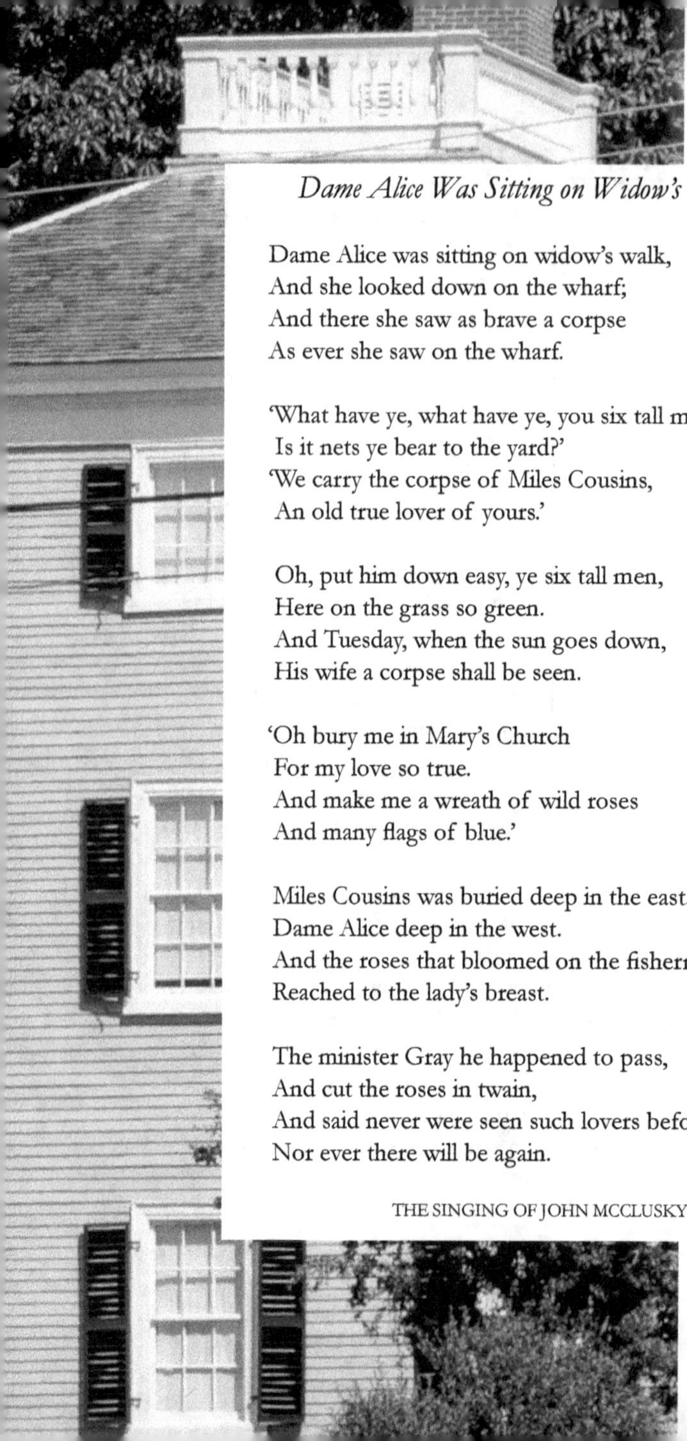

Dame Alice Was Sitting on Widow's Walk

Dame Alice was sitting on widow's walk,
And she looked down on the wharf;
And there she saw as brave a corpse
As ever she saw on the wharf.

'What have ye, what have ye, you six tall men,
 Is it nets ye bear to the yard?'
'We carry the corpse of Miles Cousins,
 An old true lover of yours.'

Oh, put him down easy, ye six tall men,
Here on the grass so green.
And Tuesday, when the sun goes down,
His wife a corpse shall be seen.

'Oh bury me in Mary's Church
For my love so true.
And make me a wreath of wild roses
And many flags of blue.'

Miles Cousins was buried deep in the east.
Dame Alice deep in the west.
And the roses that bloomed on the fisherman's grave
Reached to the lady's breast.

The minister Gray he happened to pass,
And cut the roses in twain,
And said never were seen such lovers before
Nor ever there will be again.

THE SINGING OF JOHN MCCLUSKY – EARLY 1900s

Outward Bound,
from Author's
Personal Collection

Cleopatra Barge,
from Author's
Personal Collection

Ship St. Paul,
from Author's
Personal Collection

The Mariner's Grave

Edwin Humphreys of Salem, log keeper of the ship *Ringleader*, recorded *The Mariner's Grave*[17] in the ship's journal in 1858. A similar version can be found in *American Old Time Song Lyrics* on the Traditional Music's website.[18]

I remember the night it was stormy and wet,
And dismally dashed the dark wave;
The rain and sleet, cold and heavily beat,
Round the rude dug Mariner's grave.

I remember down in a darksome dale,
And near to a dreary cave,
While the wild winds wail round the wanderer pale,
As she gazed on the Mariner's grave.

I remember how slowly the bearers trod,
How sad was the look that they gave,
As they rested their load, near its last abode,
And gazed on the Mariner's grave.

I remember a tear that slowly slid,
Down the cheeks of a messmate brave,
It fell on the lid, and soon was hid,
For closed was the Mariner's grave.

I remember no sound did the silence break
As the corpse to the earth they gave;
Save the night bids shriek or the coffin creak
As it sunk in the Mariner's grave.

Glenn Church Artist, from
Author's Personal Collection

Now o'er his lone bed the briars creep,
And wild flowers mournfully wave,
The pale moon sleeps willows weep,
On the poor lone Mariner's grave.

EDWIN HUMPHREYS, LOG KEEPER – 1858

HARRIET LOW

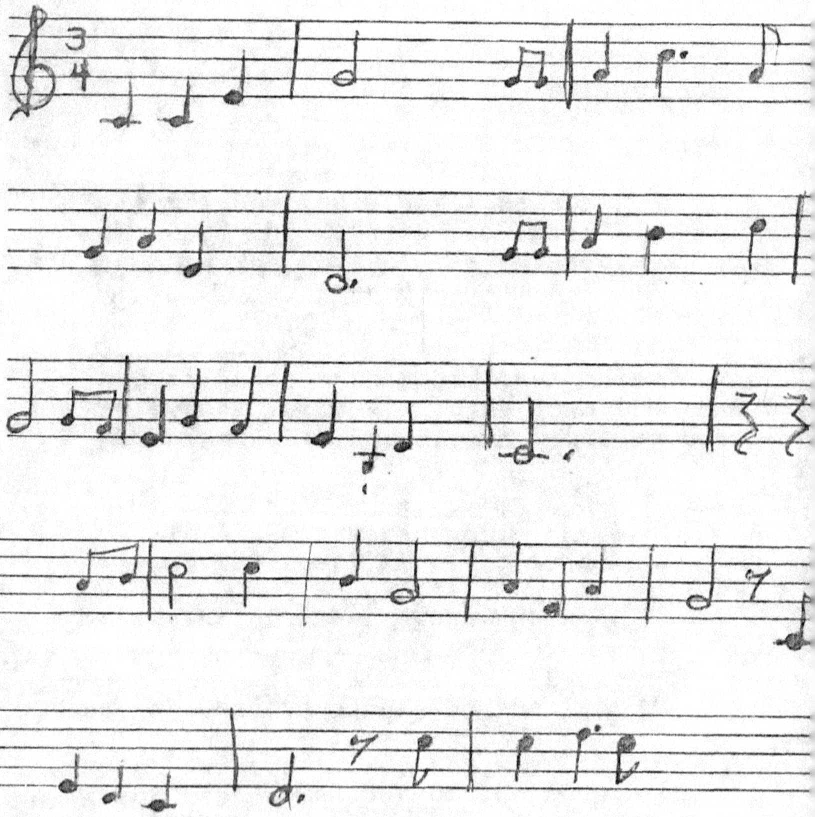

~ 6 ~

A Ship Comes In Salem

Oliver Jenkins wrote *A Ship Comes In Salem* about the town in 1830 and talks about how the "commerce situation changed much for the better" [1] between Salem and trade with the far east after the War of 1812. Born in Salem, but settled in Concord, New Hampshire, Jenkins was "raised where the salt winds blew their invigorating breaths across his face, standing as an eager little boy in old Salem, watching the sturdy seamen unload their cargoes, the sea sang its way into his soul." [2]

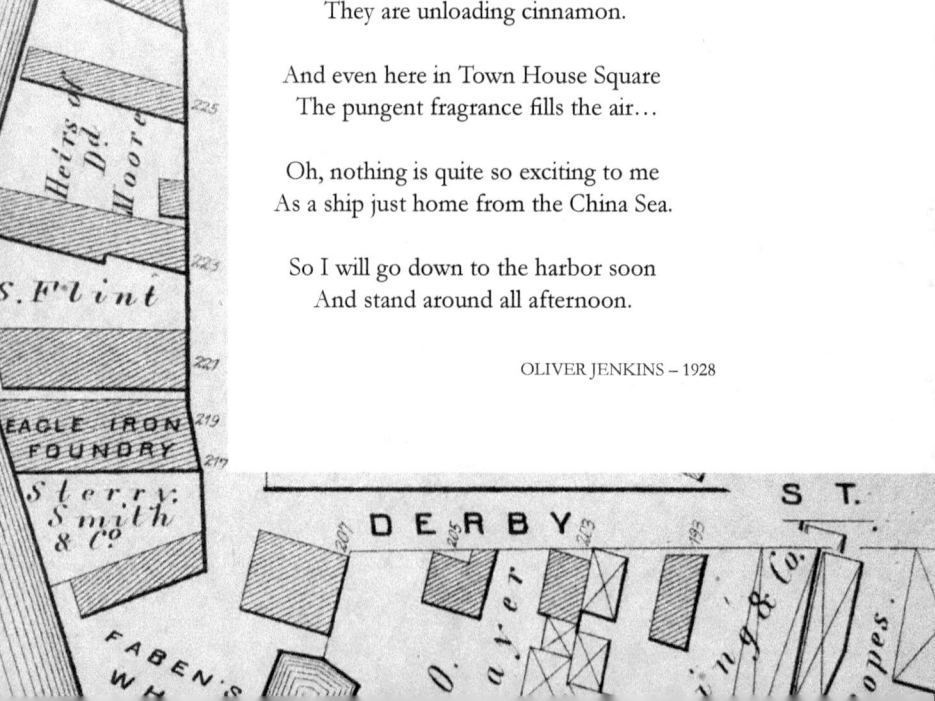

From Java, Sumatra, and old Cathay
Another ship is home today.

Now in the heat of the noonday sun
They are unloading cinnamon.

And even here in Town House Square
The pungent fragrance fills the air…

Oh, nothing is quite so exciting to me
As a ship just home from the China Sea.

So I will go down to the harbor soon
And stand around all afternoon.

OLIVER JENKINS – 1928

While Jenkins, living in New Hampshire still thinking and dreaming of old Salem. He wrote:

> I have climbed a high hill,
> Now I am coming down,
> Only a few old lights,
> Blink in the town.
>
> It was but a little way,
> And I didn't stay long:
> And yet I found a new star,
> And I learned a new song.
>
> I must have jagged rocks
> And roaring seas,
> The glint of sunlight
> On some schooner's prow, he sings. [2]

Derby Street
Salem: Present Day

Like the song, *A Ship Comes in Salem, Derby Street Salem: Present Day*,[3] was written by Oliver Jenkins He then shows how Salem has changed commercially but not for the better. Jenkins writes about Derby Street being:

> No more are the sea-chests piled high in tiers,
> Nor a trace of a spice in the wind that is blowing.

Towards the mid to late 1800s, the waterfront and the maritime trade in Salem had diminished with trade going to larger cities and deeper ports throughout the United States.

Derby Street Salem: Present Day

Never the sound of water lapping the piers
Breaks through the stillness of the daytime going:
No more are the sea-chests piled high in tiers,
Nor a trace of a spice in the wind that is blowing.

In the twilight the street lies dusty and desolate,
And overhead sea-gulls are flying, flying…
Where once calloused sailors cursed at their fate,
Dirty-faced children are crying.

Now down the harbor a horn quavers in warning
As the tide swings about and the fog comes creeping,
And all over the street until the coming morning
Drifts a mariner's chantey and a woman's weeping.

There is a challenge in a curling wave,
A challenge in a tall gaunt pine,
Even a spear of grass dancing in the wind
Is a challenge

Why do I tremble
At a grain of sand blown down the beach?

OLIVER JENKINS – 1928

Unknown Title

The son of Reverend Charles Timothy Brooks wrote this unnamed song, which he dated September 18, 1878, to commemorate the 250th Anniversary of the Landing of Governor John Endicott. The song recounts the opening of "The direct trade between Salem and Zanzibar by the *Brig Ann*." [4] The song continues on telling of the slow decline of trade for Salem ships. The ship was captained by Charles Millet and owned by Henry Prince & Son of Salem.

I was a boy when the brig Ann, a wreck,
Crawled up to Derby's wharf and landed there
Her Oriental cargo rich and rare.
What sweets and fragrances, in frails and crates,
Gum-copal, allspice, nutmegs, clover and dates!
Then filled the eyes of every Salem boy.

With mingling tears of sadness and of joy
We laughed to see how the old yellow stores
Took in the bags of sweetness through their doors;
We wept to see through what a hard fought fight
The brave old hulk had brought us such delight.
Sadly she seemed to figure as she lay,
The sunset of our old commercial day.

WORDS BY THE SON OF
REV CHARLES TIMOTHY BROOKS – 1878

Launching of the Grand Turk

The *Grand Turk* was built by the master builder Enos Briggs on the North River in Salem.[5] *The Salem Gazette* reported in the *Launching of the Grand Turk* on May 24, 1791 that "Mr. E.H. Derby requests his fellow townsmen and others to accept his sincere thanks for their ready and unwearied exertions to enable him to complete the launching of his Ship."[5] It seems that the launch was delayed for a day because of the tide. The article reads:

> Thursday last being a very pleasant day, great numbers of people assembled to see the launching of the large and beautiful ship from Mr. Derby's wharf. They were, however, disappointed in the plea sure they expected, by her stopping when she had run about half her length: and all the efforts which could be made were ineffectual in getting her off at that time, the next day.[5]

> However, with the aid of proper apparatus, and the assistance of the people assembled, she was again put in motion, and gained the water. The name of the *Grand Turk* is revived in this ship, heretofore borne by a ship belonging to Mr. Derby, remarkably successful as a privateer in the late war.[5]

The swelling waves roll joyfully along,
To greet thee, welcome to the azure main;
The gaping multitude in anxious throng,
Their ardent—vacant—tumult—scarce restrain.

Slow o'er the lubrick ways—immense—you move,
High o'er the stern your flowing honours stand,
In distant climes, on unknown seas to prove
The matchless glory of your native land.

Commerce

For thee—the lofty Cedar nods alone,
The sturdy Oak its honours lopp'd deplores,
The forest mourns its tallest beauties gone
To waft Columbian treasure—to the Indian shores.

Doom'd to resist the rage of warring waves,
Whilst rushing winds impel your foaming way:
The firm built sides their utmost fury brave,
The tempest mock—and in the whirlwind play.

Safe may you reach your distant—destin'd port
Nor rocks—nor treach'rous sands—oppose your fame,
May gentle winds your swelling topsails court,
And thousands shout you welcome home again.

TRADITIONAL – 1791

Th' Embargo

Photograph of Custom House, courtesy of Mary Barker

Th' Embargo was sung to the tune of *Oh Dear, What Can The Matter Be?* The song expressed the frustrations of the Salem merchants when selling their goods abroad. All goods coming into the country and leaving the country had to be inspected to ensure that they would only be shipped to points not included in the embargo. According to the *Salem Gazette* dated February 23, 1809, "Th' Embargo was sung on Embargo Day, in Salem, on Washington's Birthday, the song was more cheerful." [6]

Oh, dear, what can the matter be?
Dear, dear, what can the matter be?
Oh, dear, what can the matter be?
Th' Embargo's so long coming off.

It promised to make great Bonaparte humble,
It promised John Bull from his woolsack to tumble,
And not to leave either a mouthful to mumble,
At our nod to make their caps doff.

Commerce

Oh, dear, what can the matter be?
Dear, dear, what can the matter be?
Oh, dear, what can the matter be?
Th' Embargo don't answer its end.

The PEOPLE are left in the dark yet to stumble,
Their patience worn out, no wonder they grumble,
While daily they see their prosperity crumble,
And no hope their condition to mend.

Oh, dear, what can the matter be?
Dear, dear, what can the matter be?
Oh, dear, what can the matter be?
Th' Embargo don't answer its end.

TRADITIONAL – 1809

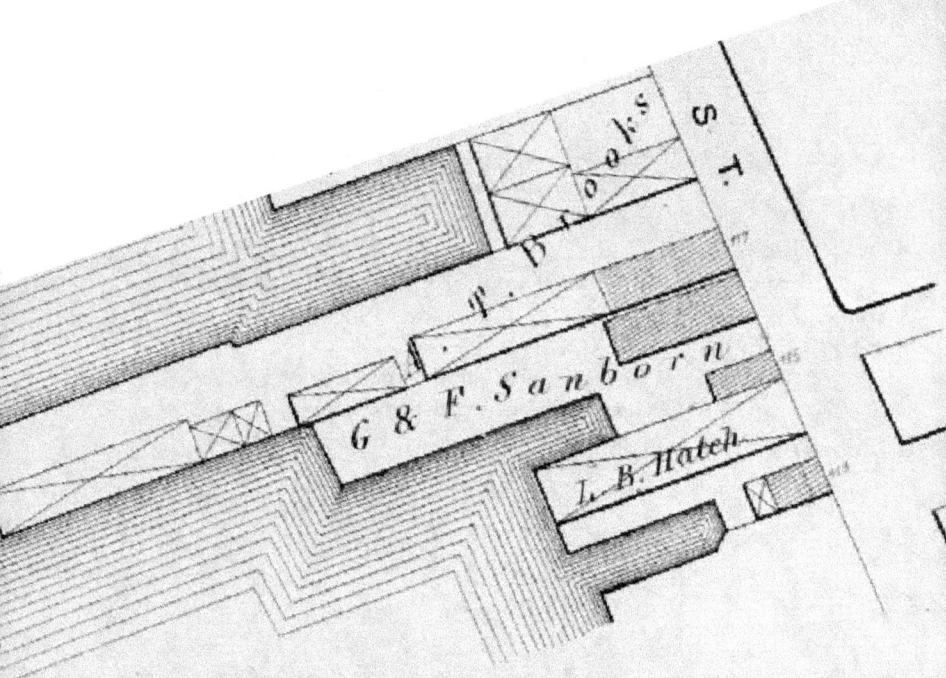

Baker's Island Light

The poem, *Baker's Island Light* [7] was found in the *Old Salem Scrap Book No. 9* by Fred A. Gannon. There is an interesting reference to the lighthouse on Baker's Island and how it guided ships into the harbor, keeping them safe.

The Skipper walked to his home by the shore and
as he walked, he looked at The light house on Baker's Island
the beacon on Nangus head.

The electric lamp on the street corner
and the candle light in his window.
And he said to himself

The light on the island has guided sailors
since the start of the nation.

So does the light of the North Star
as old as the world.

The beacon on Naugus head guides fliers in the skies.
The electric lamp on the street
guided me through the darkness.

And the light of the candle in the ancestral candlestick welcomes
me home.

Light is all about us, to guide us
and to tell us of the changes of years.
But how little do we see and understand?

TRADITIONAL – UNKNOWN

Oh Grant That Pleasant Be

Oh Grant That Pleasant Be [8] was found in the log journal #983 of the *Barque Borneo*, which called Salem homeport. While on its way to Sumatra, log keeper George Silsbee wrote:

> Sailed from Salem September 1, 1842, first into Rio de Janeiro and on Saturday eve, February 1, 1843 sailed again (after fixing the rudder) February 23, 1843 and anchored on the west bank of Sumatra, May 1, 1843. And after focusing on the cargo of pepper, September 6, 1843 bound to Gibraltar for orders. [8]

Oh grant that pleasant be our way
Over oceans broad and deep blue bed,

And brisk and free be the breeze that play
When are swelling sails are spread;

God speed us from the hidden rock,
And dangers on the wild lee shore,

God land us in tempest shock
And guide us to our house once more.

TRADITIONAL – 1842

Ye Golden Lamps of Heaven! Farewell

Philip Doddridge, an English born minister and hymn writer wrote *Ye Golden Lamps of Heaven! Farewell*. The hymn was sung at Nathaniel Bowditch's funeral to a tune written by Henry K. Oliver of Salem. Bowditch was born in Salem on March 26, 1773. At the age of ten, Bowditch was forced to leave school to work in his father's cooperage, before becoming indentured at twelve. For nine years he worked as a bookkeeping apprentice to a ship chandlery shop. [9] He was an early American mathematician remembered for his work on ocean navigation. Bowditch is credited as the founder of modern maritime navigation.

His book *The New American Practical Navigator* was first published in 1802. *The New American Practical Navigator* is still carried on board every commissioned U.S. Naval vessel.[10] Bowditch's influence on the *American Practical Navigator* was so profound that to this day mariners refer to it simply as Bowditch. In 1804, Bowditch became America's first insurance actuary and president of the Essex Fire and Marine Insurance. [10] Bowditch died in Boston on March 16, 1838 and is buried in Mt. Auburn Cemetery in Cambridge, Massachusetts.[10]

Bowditch's sextant and mariner's astrolabe are currently on display at Sail, Power, and Steam Museum [11] in Rockland Maine. Bowditch's instruments are on loan to the museum, from his decedents, who currently live in Maine. The plaque is on the Nathaniel Bowditch House and is now a National Historic Landmark and located at 9 North Street in Salem, Massachusetts.

Photograph of the Nathaniel Bowditch House, courtesy of Mary Barker

Ye golden lamps of heav'n farewell,
With all your feeble light;
Farewell thou ever-changing moon,
Pale empress of the night,

And thou refulgent orb of day,
In brighter flames arrayed;
My soul, that springs beyond thy sphere,
No more demands thy aid,

Ye stars are but the shining dust
Of my divine abode,
The pavement of those heav'nly courts,
Where I shall see my God,

The Father of eternal light
Shall there his beams display;
Nor shall one moment's darkness mix
With that unworried day.

No more the drops of pleating grief
Shall swell into mine eyes;
No more the noon-day sun decline,
Amid those brighter skies.

There all the millions of his saints
Shall in one songs unite;
And each the bliss of all shall share
Was infinite delight.

PHILIP DODDRIDGE – 1838

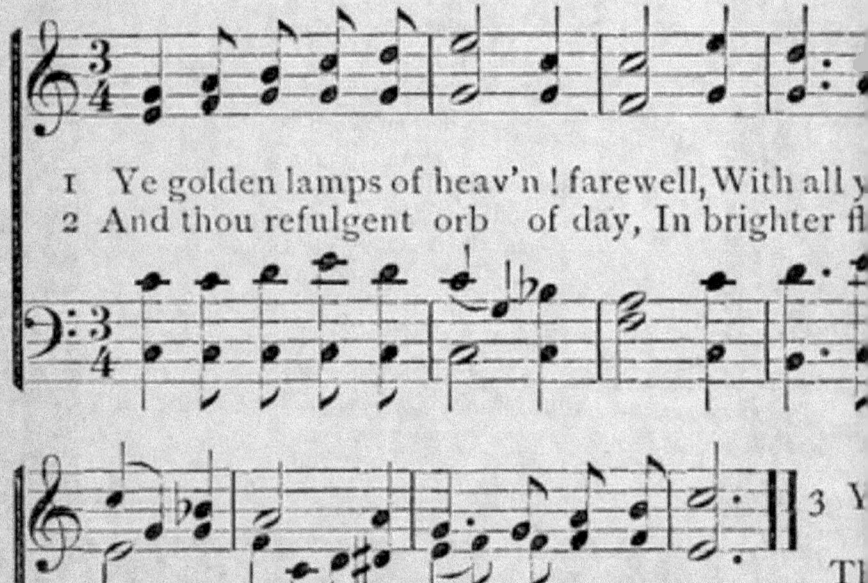

~ 7 ~
Bold Sea Captains

H. K. OLIVER

eble light ; Farewell, thou ever-
array'd ; My soul, that springs be-

s are but the shining dust
y divine abode ;
ement of those heavenly courts,
re I shall reign with God.

The Fame of Salem

The schooner *Fame* sailed out of Salem during the war of 1812. Only 70 feet in length, The *Fame* carried two guns and had a crew of 30 men. The *Fame* using her "speed and maneuverability" was one of the very first American privateers to go to sea and send home a "prize or captured vessel." [1] The song celebrates this privateer of the War of 1812. A replica of the *Fame* is now sailing out of Salem Harbor. *Ye Mariners All* [2] a local Salem folk group, recorded *The Fame of Salem* on their self-titled CD. Larry Young wrote the song with the help of John Roberts and John Rockwell. They borrowed the tune from the ballad *The Bold Richard* and added a chorus.

Now come all you brisk young Salem lads that have a mind to venture
On board a Yankee privateer, your precious lives to venture,
On board that Salem privateer, and she is called the Fame,
She's cruising out of Salem sound, bound for the Gulf of Maine.

> Chorus: Singing, What Cheer – O, aboard the Fame of Salem,
> What Cheer – O, I'll tell you all the story,
> How they fought for fame and glory,
> Singing, What Cheer – O.

Captain Webb had not sailed many leagues before he did espy
Two lofty ships a-windward, they came bearing down so nigh,
And both of them were British ships full loaded with supplies,
Webb made them haul their colors down and took them as his prize.

> Chorus: Singing, What Cheer – O, aboard the Fame of Salem,
> What Cheer – O, I'll tell you all the story,
> How they fought for fame and glory,
> Singing, What Cheer – O.

Photograph of *The Fame*, courtesy of Mary Barker

Ben Chapman took the Concord, and the Scots brig Upton got,
They took those British merchantmen and never fired a shot,
They've set a course for Salem town, their two prize ships astern,
And William Webb and his company were hailed at their return.

   Chorus: Singing, What Cheer – O, aboard the Fame of Salem,
            What Cheer – O, I'll tell you all the story,
            How they fought for fame and glory,
            Singing, What Cheer – O.

So come all you brisk young Salem lads, to the tavern we must go,
We'll sit the ladies on our knee and let the brandy flow,
And some unto their sweethearts, and some unto their wives,
And we'll sing Hallelujah to old Salem, my brave boys.

   Chorus: Singing, What Cheer – O, aboard the Fame of Salem,
            What Cheer – O, I'll tell you all the story,
            How they fought for fame and glory,
            Singing, What Cheer – O.

LARRY YOUNG – 2003

Bold Hathorne

or "The Cruise of the Fair American"

Captain Daniel Hathorne, also known as *Bold Hathorne,* [3] was the commander of the privateer *Fair American.* The ship's surgeon wrote this early American ballad about him, giving him the nickname *Bold Hathorne.* He served as a captain in the Revolutionary War and was hailed for his bravery. [4] Hathorne purchased a house in Salem in 1772 that still stands today adjacent to the House of the Seven Gables. He is also the grandfather of the well-known writer Nathaniel Hawthorne.[5]

> The twenty-second of August, before the close of day,
> All hand? On aboard our privateer, we got her under weigh;
> We kept the Eastern Shore along, for forty leagues or more,
> Then our departure took for sea, from the Isle Mohegan shore.
>
> Bold Hathorne was commander, a man of real worth,
> Old England's cruel tyranny induced him to go forth;
> She, with relentless fury, was plundering all our coast,
> And thought, because her strength was great, our glorious cause was lost.
>
> Yet boast not, haughty Britons, of power and dignity,
> Of all your conq'ring armies, your matchless strength at sea;
> Since taught by numerous instances, Americans can fight,
> With valor can equip their stand, your armies put to flight.
>
> Now farewell fair America, farewell our friends and wives,
> We trust in Heaven's peculiar care for to protect their lives,
> To prosper our intended cruise, upon the raging main.
> And to preserve our dearest friends till we return again.

We hauled up our course, and so prepared for fight;
The contest held four glasses, until the dusk of night;
Then having sprung our mainmast, and had so large a sea,
We dropped astern and left our chase till the returning day.

Next morn we fished our mainmast, the ship still being nigh,
All hands made for engaging, our luck once more to try;
But wind and sea being boisterous, our cannon would not bear,
We thought it quite imprudent, and so we left her there.

The wind it being leading, it bore us on our way,
As far unto the southward as the Gulf of Florida,
Where we observed a British ship, returning from the main;
We gave her two bow chasers, and she return'd the same.

We cruised to the eastward, near the coast of Portugal;
In longitude of twenty-seven, we saw a lofty sail:
We gave her chase and soon we saw she was a British scow,
Standing for fair America, with troops for General Howe.

Our captain did inspect her, with glasses, and he said—
"My boys, she means to fight us, but be you not afraid;
All hands now beat to quarters, see everything is clear,
We'll give her a broadside, my boys, as soon as she cornea near."

She was prepared with nettings, and had her men secured,
She bore directly for us, and put us close on board;
When cannon roar'd like thunder, and muskets fired a main,
But soon we were alongside and grappled to her chain.

And now the scene it alter'd, the cannon ceased to roar,
We fought with swords and boarding-pikes one glass or something more,
Till British pride and glory no longer dared to stay,
But cut the Yankee grappling's, and quickly bore away.

Our case was not so desperate as plainly might appear;
Yet sudden death did enter on board our privateer.
Mahoney, Crew, and Clemmons, the valiant and the brave,
Fell glorious in the contest, and met a watery grave.

Ten other men were wounded among our warlike crew,
With them our noble captain, to whom all praise is due;
To him and all our officers, let's give a hearty cheer;
Success to fair America and our good privateer!

TRADITIONAL – 1777

Hathorne is buried at the Charter Street Burying Point in Salem and the notice of his death was published in the *Salem Gazette* April 19, 1796.

In this Town, Captain Daniel Hathorne aged 65 "An honest man's noblest work of God!" and no one will doubt the deepest life to this character.

Obituary from the *Salem Gazette*, April 19, 1796

Hathorne's Gravesite, courtesy of Mary Barker

Manly
A Favorite New Song in the American Fleet

J. L. Bell, a Massachusetts writer who specializes in the start of the American Revolution in and around Boston wrote, "Of all the captains General George Washington ordered to sea in late 1775 and early 1776, one found spectacular success: John Manley. His schooner, the *Lee*, captured a string of British cargo ships in the fall of 1775, including the ordnance brig *Nancy*." [6]

Manly, A Favorite New Song in the American Fleet was composed, printed, and sold by E. Russell in Salem, Massachusetts in March 1776. The ballad refers to Captain John Manley's armed *Schooner Lee*, as a Privateer. The song is humbly addressed to all the jolly tars that are fighting for the rights and liberties of America. Captain Manley's surname may have been deliberately misspelled in the song title in order to rally men for war. [7]

BRAVE MANLY he is stout, and his Men have proved true,
By taking of those English ships, he makes their Jacks to rue;
To our Ports he sends their Ships and Men, let's give a hearty Cheer
To Him and all those valiant Souls who go in Privateers.

> Chorus: And a privateering we will go, my boys, my Boys,
> And a Privateering we will go.

O all ye gallant Sailor Lads, don't never be dismay'd,
Nor let your Foes in Battle ne'er think you are afraid,
Those dastard Sons shall tremble when our Cannon they do roar,
We'll take, or sink, or burn them all, or them we'll drive on Shore

> Chorus: And a privateering we will go, my boys, my Boys,
> And a Privateering we will go.

Our Heroes they're not daunted when Cannon Balls do fly,
For we're resolv'd to conquer, or bravely we will die;
Then rouse all you NEW-ENGLAND Oaks, give MANLY now a Cheer,
Likewise those Sons of Thunder who go in Privateers.

> Chorus: And a privateering we will go, my boys, my Boys,
> And a Privateering we will go.

Their little petty Pirates our Coast shall ne'er infest,
We'll catch their sturdy Ships, Boys, for those we do like best;
Then enter now my hearty Lads, the War is just begun,
To make our Fortunes at their Cost, we'll take them as they run.

> Chorus: And a privateering we will go, my boys, my Boys,
> And a Privateering we will go.

While Shuldham he is flying from WASHINGTON's strong Lines,
Their Troops and Sailors run for fear, and leave their Stores behind
Then rouse up, all our Heroes, give MANLY now a Cheer,
Here's a Health to hardy Sons of Mars who go in Privateers.

> Chorus: And a privateering we will go, my boys, my Boys,
> And a Privateering we will go.

They talk of Sixty Ships, Lads, to scourge our free-born Land,
If they send out Six Hundred we'll bravely them withstand;
Resolve we thus to conquer, Boys, or bravely we will die,
In fighting for our Wives and Babes, as well as LIBERTY.

> Chorus: And a privateering we will go, my boys, my Boys,
> And a Privateering we will go.

Bold Sea Captains

I pray you Landsmen enter, you'll find such charming Fun,
When to our Ports by Dozens their largest Ships they come;
Then make your Fortunes now, my Lads, before it is too late
Defend, defend, I say defend an INDEPENDENT STATE.

   Chorus: And a privateering we will go, my boys, my Boys,
       And a Privateering we will go.

While the Surf it is tossing and Cannon Balls do fly,
We surely will our Foes subdue, or cheerfully will die,
Then rouse, all you bold Seamen, brave MANLY's COMMODORE
Should we meet with our desp'rate Foes, bless us, they will be tore,

   Chorus: And a privateering we will go, my boys, my Boys,
       And a Privateering we will go.

Then cheer up, all my hearty Souls, to Glory let us run,
Where Cannon Balls do rattle, with sounding of the Drum;
For who would Cowards prove, or even stoop to Fear,
When MANLY he commands us in our bold PRIVATEER.

   Chorus: And a privateering we will go, my boys, my Boys,
       And a Privateering we will go.

While HOPKINS he is trimming them upon the Southern Shore,
We'll scour our Northern Coast, Boys, as soon as they come o'er;
Then rouse up, all my Hearties, give Sailor Lads a Cheer,
Brave MANLY, HOPKINS, and those Tars who go in Privateers.

   Chorus: And a privateering we will go, my boys, my Boys,
       And a Privateering we will go.

                 E. RUSSELL – 1776

Billy Taylor

The song *Billy Taylor* was culled from the *Salem Gazette*. The article *Impressment* and the song from the Gazette was dated March 30, 1813, and states that this song came from the *Connecticut Mirror*. The *Salem Gazette* printed the song as written from the Mirror, and how Billy Taylor was "Prest and he went to sea." [8] Billy Taylor's lover then follows him to sea dressed in sailor's clothes. After being discovered on board, she tells the Captain: "Kind sir, I've cum to seek my true love, whom you press'd and sent to sea."

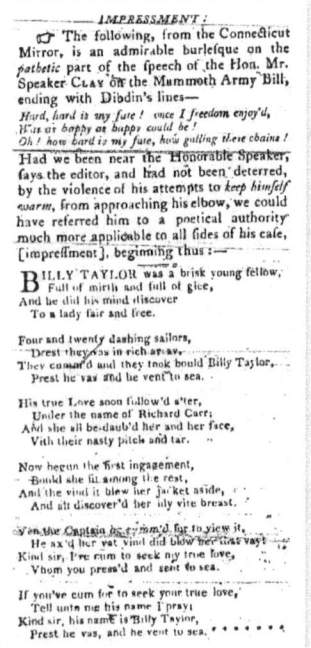

Impressment! Salem Gazette, March 30, 1813

Impressment! Salem Gazette, April 12, 1813

136

Billy Taylor

Billy Taylor was a brisk young fellow
Full of mirth and full of glee
And he did his mind discover
To a lady fair and free.

Four and twenty dashing sailors
Drest they were in rich array
They comm'd and they took Billy Taylor
Prest he was and he went to sea.

His true love soon follow'd a'ter
Under the name of Richard Carr
And she all daub'd her and her face
With their nasty pitch and tar.

Now begun the first engagement,
Bold she fit among the rest
And the wind it blew her jacket aside
And all discover'd her lily white breast

When the captain he runn'd for to view it
He ax'd her what wind did blow her dress away
Kind sir, I've cum to seek my true love,
Whom you press'd and sent to sea.

If you cum for to seek your true love,
Tell me unto his name I pray,
Kind sir, his name is Billy Taylor
Prest he was and he went to sea.

Two weeks later a gentleman wrote to the *Salem Gazette* and his rebuttal was printed in the Gazette on April 12, 1813 stating:

> but I am inclined to think it would not have been adopted because the case of Billy Taylor turned out at last, like many of the pretended cases of impressment -- as many were not on board---, likewise one reason why impressed seamen, have not been heard from, as you will see by the other part of the song. [9]

The writer added four additional verses that were printed in the Gazette. The woman in disguise begins explaining her reasoning for being on board and that she was looking for her supposedly impressed lover, Billy Taylor. The Captain stated: "And you will find him in London streets, ma'am, walking with his lady gay." She leaves the ship to find her lover on the street. She approaches him as he was walking with another women, and shoots him dead. The Captain applauded her for what she had done and rewarded her by making her a First Lieutenant.

Billy Taylor (continued)

If you be kin'd for to seek your true love
He from the ship is gone away
And you will find him in London streets, ma'am,
Walking with his lady gay.

She rose up early the next morning
Long before 'Twas the break of day,
And she found false Billy Taylor
Walking with his lady gay.

Straight she call'd for swords and pistols-
Fetched they was at her command-
She fell a-shooting Billy Taylor
With his lady in his hand

When for the Captain he kindly for to know it,
He very much applauded her for what she had done,
And he made her First Lieutenant
Of the valiant Thunder Bomb.

TRADITIONAL – PRE 1800

The *Essex Register*, a local Salem newspaper, dated April 7, 1813 reported that the United States government has received reports of 6,257 cases of impressments and believes that only one third of the impressments have been reported. The government also believes that one eighth of the seamen in the British Navy are Americans.[10] The British reported that only ten men from Salem have been impressed but the U.S. government has unofficial reports of possibility as many as 150 men. The known impressed seamen were listed in an article in the *Essex Register* dated April 10, 1813. The list began at No. 91, indicating that every so often the newspaper prints know impressed sailors from Salem. Below is a partial list of sailors:

No. 91. William Collet from ship *Recovery* of Salem.
No. 92. John Gale impressed from the same ship.
No. 93. James Mitchell of the ship *Recovery*.
No. 94. John Russell of the ship *Recovery*.
No. 95. Lewis Langdon sailed on the ship *America*.
No. 96. John Coffin from the schooner *Two Brothers*.
No. 97. Joseph West impressed from the *Brig Wm. & Charles*.
   (List to be continued) [11]

The Battle of Quallah Battoo

The Battle of Quallah Battoo was found in the *Essex Institute Historical Collection* called *Salem Vessels and Their Voyages: A History of the Pepper Trade with the Island of Sumatra.* [12]

The National Park Service of Salem states on their website that, the original *Friendship* was built for the Salem firm, Waite, and Pierce in the South River shipyard of Enos Briggs and was first launched in 1797. The *Friendship* made 15 voyages during her career until the British *Sloop HMS Rosamond* captured her as a prize of war on September 5, 1812. [13, 14]

The Friendship as she was leaving Gloucester after being repaired and returning to Salem in 2019, courtesy of Mary Barker

Pierce and Waite built a second ship in 1815 with the same name. This new *Friendship* was constructed in Portland, Maine, and registered at the Customs House in Salem on January 6, 1816. Three years later she was sold to George Nichols, Ichabod Nichols, Benjamin Pierce, Henry Pierce, and Charles Saunders. In 1827, Dudley L. Pickman, Nathaniel Silsbee, William Zachariah Silsbee, and Richard F. Stone purchased the vessel and hired the vessel for the pepper trade. [14]

The Battle of Quallah Battoo

The sun was retiring behind the high mountains,
The forts of our enemy full in our view;
The frigate Potomac, John Downes, our commander,
Rode proudly at anchor, off Quallah Battoo.

The land breeze blew mild, the night was serene
Our boats was the word and our tackles were mann'd;
Six miles was the distance that now lay between
Our fine lofty ship and the enemy's land.

Our boats were launch'd on the breast of the billows,
And moor'd till the word of command should be given;
On deck we reposed with our swords for our pillows,
And committed our cause, with its justness, to Heaven.

At the dead hour of night, when all nature was silent,
The boatswain's shrill pipe call'd each man to his post;
Our hearts arm'd with justice, our minds fully bent
To attack and destroy that piratical host.

Who boarded the Friendship, and murder'd her crew,
Just twelve months before the memorable day,
When Shubrick led forth the Potomac's so true,
To fight and to vanquish the hostile Malay.

Our boats were all ready, and we were prepared
To fight or to die, for our cause it was just;
Our muskets were loaded, and our bosoms were bared
To the strife or the storm, for in God was our trust.

When thus spoke our brave and respected commander,
"I charge you by all that is sacred below,
From the true paths of honour, or virtue, ne'er wander;
If mercy's requested, then mercy bestow.

Never let it be said, that the sons of Columbia,
Sheath'd their swords in the breast of a female or child;
And may virtue and honour attend you this day;
Be you death to the arm'd, to the helpless be mild.

Now silence and darkness prevail'd all around,
We left the Potomac, and steer'd for the shore;
Save the noise of the sea-beach, we heard not a sound,
Our rowlocks were matted, and muffled each oar.

The white surf ran high, as our boats near'd the strand,
And the gray streaks of morning began to appear;
But, by prudence and caution, we safely did land,
Though the waters were wild and the enemy near.

To their force, to their arms, to their strength, we were strangers,
    But bravely advanced to the forts of our foe;
We thought of no trouble, we thought of no dangers,
    Determined, unless we in death were laid low.

To revenge the sad wrongs that our friends and our nation
    So oft have sustain'd from those demons of hell;
Our work we commenced, and the bright conflagration,
    Left but few of our foes the sad story to tell.

Their forts, they were strong, and like heroes they fought,
    For mercy or quarter they never had shown;
And the blood of their victims forever they sought,
    But the God of the Christians they never had known.

All around us in ambush those savages lay,
    And the bullets like hail-stones were scattered abroad.
But still on their forts we continued to play,
    To conquer our object, Potomac's our word.

Exposed to their fires, the Potomac's advanced,
    Beneath their rude ramparts stood firmly and brave;
Resolved that the stripes and stars of Columbia
    E're long on their ramparts triumphant should wave.

Their firing soon ceased, and our brave pioneers
    Then opened a path, and we entered their gates;
We paused but a moment, gave three hearty cheers,
    Then hoisted the flag that is worn by the states.

The white dashing surf now began to increase,
And warn'd us the hour of departure was near;
Our wounded and slain we collected in peace,
And form'd, with our pikes and our muskets, a bier.

To convey them, all weltering and pale, from the shore
　To our ship, that majestically rode on the wave;
　To comfort the wounded, the dead to deplore,
　And commit their remains to a watery grave.

The Potomac, victorious, once more under way,
Floats proudly along the smooth eastern waters;
Columbia! Columbia! The deeds of that day
Shall be told by thy sons, and be sung by thy daughters.

Our officers, valiant in battle or war,
In the calm time of peace they are generous and kind;
Our crew for the brave and American Star
Are all in one voice and one body combin'd.

May success then attend us, wherever we roam,
And nothing our cause or our progress impede;
May the Potomac, with glory and honour come home,
And her name ne'er be stain'd with an unworthy deed.

WRITTEN BY ONE OF THE CREW – 1832

Captain Charles Endicott sailed the *Friendship* to the island of Sumatra in 1831 in search of pepper. The Malays at Quallah Battoo attacked the *Friendship* of Salem off the coast of Sumatra. The ship was captured on February 7th while Captain Endicott was on shore to purchase and weigh pepper. [15] When Captain Endicott and the other officers heard the news, they tried to return to the *Friendship* to aid the crew, but were unsuccessful. They made their way to where the American vessels *James Monroe, Palmer,* and *Governor Endicott* were lying at anchor. "Once the captains of these vessels heard Endicott's story they hauled anchor and set sail to recover the *Friendship*." [16]

Endicott returned to Salem. There was a public outcry and President Andrew Jackson dispatched the *USS Potomac* under Captain John Downers to "punish the natives for their treachery." [17]

The Friendship and the *Adventure* in dry-dock, (2018) Gloucester Massachusetts, courtesy of Mary Barker

Peace Party

The *Peace Party* is from the Isaiah Thomas Broadside Ballads Project. Stephen G. Clark was commander of the *Schooner Castigator*, out of Salem. On August 3, 1813 the *Castigator* was detained outside of Boston Harbor for capturing the British *Brig Dispatch* and taking their cargo of wine and merchandise, [18] even though they had a letter of marque from the president of the United States. The ship's letter of marque stated, "against the vessels, goods, and efforts of the government of the United Kingdom." [18] Court proceeding followed and the *Castigator* was eventually allowed to keep the goods and sell them in accordance with their letter of marque. This incident became known as the "Battle of the Peace Party."

Capture of the Brig Dispatch, Part I
Salem Gazette, August 6, 1813

Peace Party

COME all ye noble warriors,
Who delight in blood and scars?
And hear a simple ditty,
But not of foreign wars.

In Boston Town are many,
Who have much gold in store?
But yet they are so craving,
They put to sea for more.

No matter where it comes from,
So the money they but get,
And sure 'tis true as gospel,
They've money more than wit.

Relying on Old BRITAIN,
They send their ships to sea,
To feed their country's haters,
And fill their hearts with glee.

JOHN BULL full well rewards them,
And freights their ships with gold,
And stocks, like KID the pirate,
With "dollars manifold."

Now from her voyage returning,
A FEDERAL Brig we spy,
A FEDERAL CASTIGATOR
Now has her in her eye,

"Lay to" says CASTIGATOR,
"Ay! Ay!', says Miss DESPATCH
And without leave or LICENCE,
The LICENC'D ship they catch,

When near FORT INDEPENDENCE,
'Twas there, O ! sad mischance,
A Yankee Bull-DOG bark'd out,
And bid them stop their dance,

Next day to bar of Justice,
(They little of it thought,)
The leaders of these heroes,
By officers were brought.

When first they hear the tidings,
The owners rave and swear,
Resolve to be revenged,
And pull the captor's hair,

Then out two boats are fitted,
With forty men well arm'd,
The enterprise is novel,
And with it they are charm'd.

Now down the harbor steering,
The Brig they soon espy,
The CASTIGATOR by her
Their force seems to defy.

Some shots were now exchanged,
But they no limbs did break,
And soon these valiant heroes,
Jump'd on the vessels, deck.

They took complete possession,
To Boston steer'd their way,
Well pleas'd, that without bloodshed,
They'd bravely won the day.

The Lawyers search'd their volumes,
To find their crime did try,
THIS Lawyer call'd them pirates,
That, 'together did deny.

The Judge then gravely told 'em,
This cause we sure must try it,
And for the sake of shortness
We'll set it down "A RIOT."

So they were then bound over,
To answer to the laws,
For shooting guns and pistols,
Without sufficient cause.

Now privateer and boatmen,
(As it has since turn'd out,)
Were all of the "Peace-Party,"
Who made this noise and rout.

No more let these mild gentry,
Of mobs in Baltimore,
Curse out, and swear, and bellow,
But all such trash give o'er.

Now let all the "PEACE PARTY,"
By this a warning take,
And not like foolish children,
Try each other's heads to break.

TRADITIONAL – 1813

The Peace Party was a group in the United States that did not agree with President Madison and wanted the United States government to negotiate with England rather than taking up arms.

Yesterday, the privateersmen, nine in number, found on board the brig, were taken into custody, and arraigned before the civil authority of the state; and after a short examination some were recognized, and the others committed. The investigation will be continued this day. It is ascertained that the privateer boats, by which the Dispatch was detained, were fitted out at Salem.

Capture of the Brig Dispatch, Part II
Salem Gazette, August 6, 1813

Occasioned by the arrival of the remains of
Lawrence and Ludlow at Salem

The ballad *Occasioned by the arrival of the remains of Lawrence and Ludlow at Salem* is from the book, *An account of the funeral honours bestowed on the remains of Captain Lawrence and Lieutenant Ludlow.* [19] Captain Lawrence sailed his ship *Chesapeake* and its green and untrained crew directly at the English *Brig Shannon* near Boston Light. The battle lasted for only fifteen minutes. Both Captain Lawrence and Lieutenant Ludlow were mortally wounded. Captain Lawrence's last words were, 'Don't give up the ship!' This phrase is still used in the Navy today. [20] The *Shannon* then sailed with the *Chesapeake* to Halifax, Nova Scotia. "There, Lawrence and his next senior officer, Lieutenant Augustus C. Ludlow, were buried with full military honors." [20]

RELICS of the fallen brave!
Tenants of an honor'd tomb!
Conscious pride exalts the wave
Whose swelling bosom bears you home.

Ocean hails you, gallant souls!
Now once more his realm you cross;
And each billow as it rolls,
Moans an anthem for your loss.

Glory's halo binds your brows.
Immortality is your shroud,
While our love, like zephyr, blows
From your disk of fame, each cloud.

Adoration warms the clay
That was cold on foreign men

Our best sacrifice we pay,
'Tis the silent, grief swol'n tear.

Sons of Glory! Mighty Dead!
Welcome to your parent land;
Softly here shall rest your head,
Pillow'd by your brothers' hand.

Lawrence! Ludlow! Sons of Fame!
Here shall rise the sculptured stone.
"Noble is the Hero's name,
Glory claims it as her own!

TRADITIONAL – 1813

Captain Crowinshield of Salem did not want Captain Lawrence and Lieutenant Ludlow's remains in Halifax. He wrote a letter to Secretary of State, James Monroe, asking for permission to, at his own expense, to retrieve the "gallant body of Captain Lawrence and have him buried in the United States." [19] The *Brig Henry* with Crowinshield and his crew sailed from Salem to Halifax on August 7, 1813 with a flag of truce. On August 13th, Crowinshield sailed back to Salem with the remains of Captain Lawrence and Lieutenant Ludlow on board. [19] Captain Lawrence and Lieutenant Ludlow were buried in Salem for a short period of time. Their bodies were exhumed once more and buried at their final resting place at Trinity Church in New York.

Funeral of Capt. Lawrence and Lt. Ludlow, *Essex Register*, Saturday, August 21, 1813 [21]

The Loss off (of) Sir John Franklin

The Loss off (of) Sir John Franklin was written in the logbook of the ship *Ringleader*[22] out of Boston. Edwin Humphrey of Salem was the log keeper and wrote down this version in 1858. This ballad is about Captain Sir John Franklin's fatal voyage on the *Erebus* and *Terror* to find a northwest passage to the Pacific Ocean from England. Robert B. Waltz stated in *The Traditional Ballad Index* at Fresno State that an early version of this ballad was found in 1861 and written in the journal of the *Morning Light*.[23] The original version was probably written circa 1851 – 52. There are several broadside versions of *Lady Franklin's Lament* found on The Bodleian Library Broadside Ballad collection website.[24] Each version is slightly different but a similar version to the *The Loss off (of) Sir John Franklin* is called *Lady Franklin's Lament for her Husband*, Roud Number 487.

The Loss off (of) Sir John Franklin

Young seamen bold who have with stood
The storms that rose over the mighty flood
Attend these lines, which I shall name
It will but you in mind of a sufferers dream.

As homeward bound on the mighty deep
Lay in my hammock a fast a sleep
I had a dream, which I thought was true
Concerning Franklin and his ship's crew.

As we passed by the artic shore
I heard a lady she did deplore
She wept aloud and seemed to say
Alas my Franklin is far away

Bold Sea Captains

It is long since a ship of fame
That bore my Franklin over the main
With one hundred seamen bold and stout
To find a northwest passage out.

To find a passage around the North Pole
Where the lightning flash and loud thunder roll
Its more than mortal man can do
With hearts undaunted and courage due.

Now sad foreboding does give me pain
Since my long last Franklin has crossed the main
Ten thousand pounds I'll freely give
So now on earth that my Franklin lives.

Seven long years has passed and gone
Blows many a keen and wintery storm
Blows over the grave where poor seamen fell,
Those fate and sufferings no tongue can tell.

There's Capt. Kerry of Seaburn town
Cownwells & (Rivers) of high renown
There is Capt. Ross and many more
Long time been cruising the Artic Shore.

They sailed East, they sailed West
Along Greenland shores where they thought best
Through toils and dangers they manly stood
Till mountainous Icebergs there ships where ....

In Baffin Bay where the whale fish blows
The fate of Franklin no one doth knows
But alas he like many more
Who have left their home to return no more.

EDWIN HUMPHREY – 1858

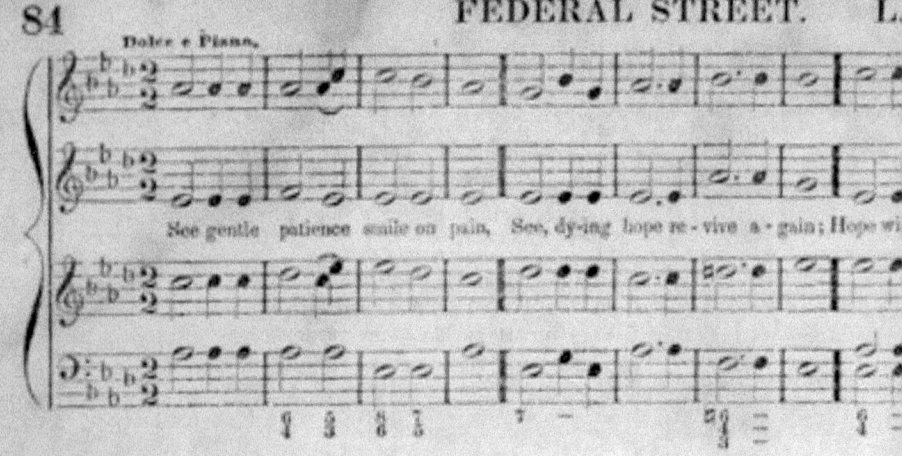

~ 8 ~
Captain Edward B. Trumbull

Captain Edward B. Trumbull

Captain Edward B. Trumbull of Salem, Massachusetts lived at 90 Federal Street. The house was built in 1887 for Annie Bertram Webb and for many years (1896 - 1935) was the home of Trumbull. Captain Trumbull was a shipmaster and one of the last foreign trade sea captains to sail out of Salem.[1]

Captain Trumbull engaged in the East Coast of Africa trade as master of the *Bark Taria Topan*.[2] The *Taria Topan* was launched on April 2, 1870 from Edward F. Miller's boatyard in south Salem. The ship was the last vessel of any size belonging to Salem owners and built in Salem.[3]

Captain Edward B. Trumbull, courtesy of the Salem Marine Society

Between the years 1927 - 1928 Captain Trumbull gave James Carpenter seventeen sea songs and sea shanties that he learned while captain of the *Taria Topan*. Carpenter collected these songs from Trumbull and others while researching for his thesis.

James Carpenter is from Mississippi and attended Harvard University in 1920. While at Harvard, he met George Lyman Kittredge, a leading literary scholar and folklorist. Carpenter worked on his thesis entitled *Forecastle Songs and Chanties* and gained his doctorate in 1929 from Harvard University.[4]

Each song from the Carpenter Collection that was collected by Captain Trumbull is included in this book. Carpenter's thesis is presently housed at the Library of Congress.

Captain Edward B. Trumbull

The song below is a partial example of Trumbull's version of an old sea shanty. *Captain Trumbull* [5] is better known as *Haul Away Joe*. Two verses have been left out on the shanty because of offensive language.

Captain Trumbull

Away, haul away,
Haul away my Josie!

Away, Haul away,
Haul away my Joe!

Oh once I had a Yankee girl
And she was tall and spunky;

Away, Haul away,
Haul away my Joe!

TRADITIONAL – 1868

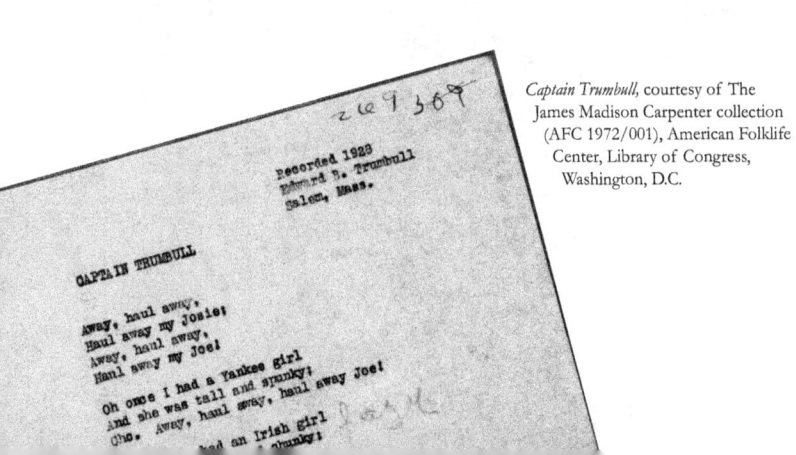

Captain Trumbull, courtesy of The James Madison Carpenter collection (AFC 1972/001), American Folklife Center, Library of Congress, Washington, D.C.

The Salem Marine Society was organized by captains and ship owners in 1766 to share navigation information and to provide benefits for needy members and their families. The Marine Society agreed to raze the Franklin Building (the society's meeting place) and sell the land in order to build the Hawthorne Hotel. [6] In exchange, the hotel built a room for the society to use on the top floor. Captain Edward B. Trumbull helped to design a unique room on the top floor of the Hawthorne Hotel in Salem, Massachusetts. The once-secret room was 'soaked in the legacy of the sea and the ships' captains who sailed into history. A replica of the deckhouse aboard the *Taria Topan*, Trumbull's last command, was built as the meeting place for the Marine Society at Salem.

Boston Traveler, Friday, August 28, 1925, courtesy of the Boston Public Library

Captain Edward B. Trumbull

Salem Marine Society's Room and Hawthorne Hotel, from Author's Personal Collection

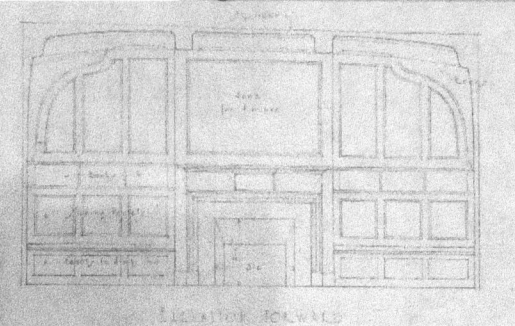

Architect's drawing of the Salem Marine Society's forward wall with Captain Trumbull's approval signature, courtesy of the Salem Marine Society

Tom Pepper

Carpenter wrote in his notes about the song *Tom Pepper*, "*Tom Pepper* is synonymous with "greatest liar." For the perfect blending of a spirited, swinging tune with words wholly given over to rollicking fun. I have not seen it surpassed." [7] The song was recorded by Carpenter in 1927 and was learned by Trumbull sometime between 1868 and 1874. Bob Walser made a recording of *Tom Pepper* on his CD, *Outward Bound on the J.M Carpenter: Songs from the James Madison Carpenter Collection* in 2018.

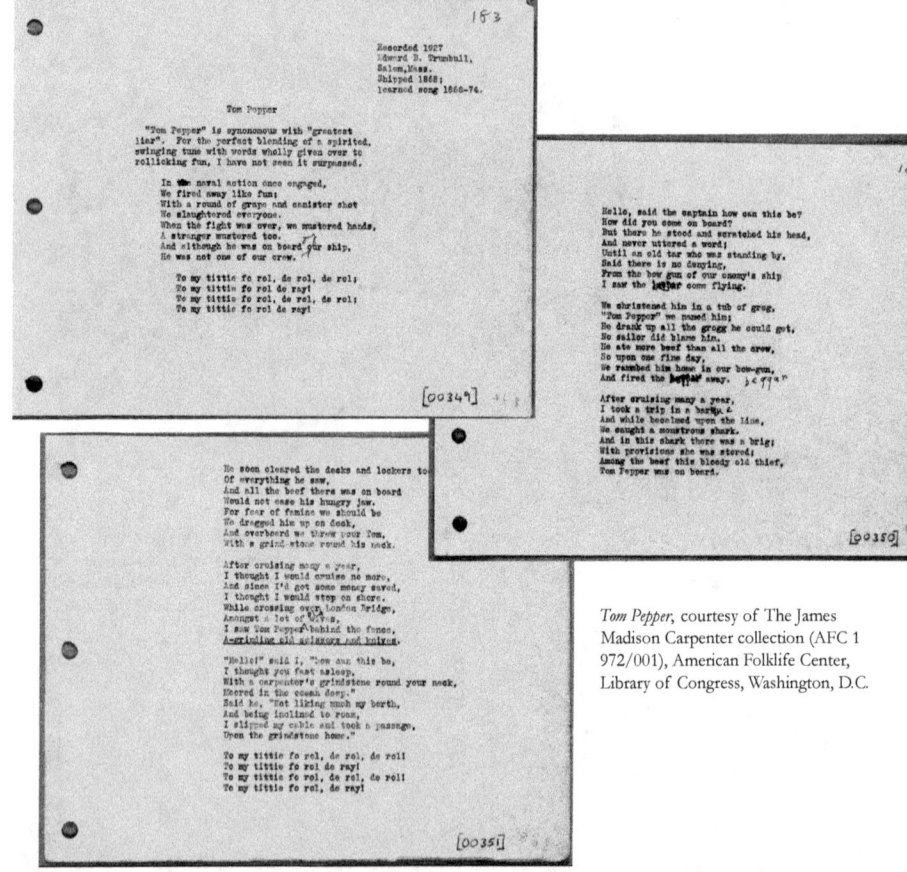

Tom Pepper, courtesy of The James Madison Carpenter collection (AFC 1 972/001), American Folklife Center, Library of Congress, Washington, D.C.

Tom Pepper

In the naval action once engaged,
We fired away like fun;
With a round of grape and canister shot
We slaughtered everyone.
When the fight was over we mustered hands,
A stranger mustered too.
And although he was on board of our ship;
He was not one of our crew.

Chorus: To my tittie fo rol, de rol, de rol;
         To my tittie fo rol de ray!
         To my tittie fo rol, de rol, de rol;
         To my tittie fo rol de ray!

Hello, said the captain, how can this be?
How did you come on board?
But there he stood and scratched his head,
And never uttered a word;
Until an old tar who was standing by,
Said there is no denying,
From the bow gun of our enemy's ship
I saw the beggar come flying.

Chorus: To my tittie fo rol, de rol, de rol;
         To my tittie fo rol de ray!
         To my tittie fo rol, de rol, de rol;
         To my tittie fo rol de ray!

We christened him in a tub of grog,
'Tom Pepper' we named him;
He drank up all the grog he could get,
No sailor did blame him.

He ate more beef than all the crew,
So upon one fine day,
We rammed him home in our bow-gun,
And fire the beggar away.

Chorus: To my tittie fo rol, de rol, de rol;
        To my tittie fo rol de ray!
        To my tittie fo rol, de rol, de rol;
        To my tittie fo rol de ray!

After cruising many a year,
I took a trip in a barque;
And while becalmed upon the line,
We caught a monstrous shark.
And in this shark there was a brig;
With provisions she was stored;
Among the beef this bloody old thief,
Tom Pepper was on board.

Chorus: To my tittie fo rol, de rol, de rol;
        To my tittie fo rol de ray!
        To my tittie fo rol, de rol, de rol;
        To my tittie fo rol de ray!

He soon cleared the decks and lockers too,
Of everything he saw,
And all the beef there was on board
Would not ease his hungry jaw.
For fear of famine we should be
We dragged him up on deck,
And overboard we threw poor Tom,
With a grindstone around his neck.

Chorus: To my tittie fo rol, de rol, de rol;
        To my tittie fo rol de ray!
        To my tittie fo rol, de rol, de rol;
        To my tittie fo rol de ray!

After cruising many a year,
I thought I would cruise no more,
And since I'd got some money saved,
I thought I would stop on shore.
While crossing over London Bridge,
Amongst a lot of old wives,
I saw Tom Pepper behind the fence,
A-grinding old scissors and knives.

Chorus: To my tittie fo rol, de rol, de rol;
        To my tittie fo rol de ray!
        To my tittie fo rol, de rol, de rol;
        To my tittie fo rol de ray!

"Hello!" said I, "how can this be,
I thought you were fast asleep,
With a carpenter's grindstone round your neck,
Moored in the ocean deep."
Said he, "Not liking much my breath,
And being inclined to roam,
I slipped my cable and took a passage,
Upon the grindstone home.

Chorus: To my tittie fo rol, de rol, de rol;
        To my tittie fo rol de ray!
        To my tittie fo rol, de rol, de rol;
        To my tittie fo rol de ray!

TRADITIONAL – 1868 - 1874

Kizee Makazee-Yah

Kizee Makazee - Yah is a work song written down by Captain Trumbull in his log journal #1056 on a trip to Zanzibar on the *Barque Taria Topan* out of Salem in 1886. The song referred to a sailing vessel getting unloaded, on Cape Kizee Makazee, the south end of Zanzibar Island. [8] Trumbull states:

> The mate in charge of the deck, where he has about three of the crew to take the most important places and a string of (locals) to hoist out the cargo. About 20 or 30 string onto a rope, which is led through a leading block, hooked to a bolt in the rail. They run along the deck, singing a song of their own making in English. [8]

Trumbull recounts that they would sing this work song from the time they came on board in the morning until they go on shore at night, every day and every voyage; "I had it by heart, and have never forgotten it." [8] According to Captain Trumbull's report, the chanting rhythm of the local natives had "a high degree of force and stimulation." [9]

Kizee Makazee - Yah

White manee, he no savey,
Kizee Makazee - Ho!
White manee, he no savey,
Kizee Makazee - Ho!

TRADITIONAL – 1886
FROM TRUMBULL'S LOG BOOK #1

Captain Edward B. Trumbull

Zanzibar Work Song

White manee, he no savey,
Kizee Makazee, wa-a-ah!
White manee, he no savey,
Kizee Makazee - yah!

TRADITIONAL – 1886
FROM CARPENTER'S INTERVIEW
WITH TRUMBULL IN 1927

Sally Brown [10]

Sally muzzles all my payday;
Away, roll and go.
How I love my pretty Sally!
Spent my money on Sally Brown!

Sally Brown, I'm bound to leave you,
Away, roll and go.
Sally Brown, I'll ne'er forget you.
Spent my money on Sally Brown!

So shake her up and let her go, sir;
Away, roll and go.
Pretty soon I'll be back with her.
Spent my money on Sally Brown!

Sally brown, she is my darling,
Away, roll and go.
Sally brown, she is my darling,
Spent my money on Sally Brown!

TRADITIONAL – 1868

Blow The Man Down

A version of *Blow the Man Down* was made popular from the singing of *Popeye* on Saturday morning cartoons. *Blow the Man Down* was recorded with Billy Costello providing the voice of Popeye in 1935. [11] Trumbull's version mentions leaving Boston town for Mobile Bay to load and deliver cotton. The work was hard and towards the end of the song, the sailors sing, "I wish I was in Boston town." [12] The sailors wishing they were home drinking gin with their Boston girls.

There was an old man and his name it was Brown,
    Wa-a-ay, blow the man down!
They say he hailed from Boston town,
    Give us some time to blow the man down!

We're bound away this very day,
    Wa-a-ay, blow the man down!
We're bound away to Mobile Bay,
    Give us some time to blow the man down!

Recorded 1927
Captain Edward B. Tru[mbull]
Salem, Massachusetts
First shipped 1868

BLOW THE MAN DOWN

There was an old man and his name it was Brown;
Wa-a-ay, blow the man down!
They say he hailed from Boston town;
Give us some time to blow the man down!

We're bound away this very day;
We're bound away to Mobile Bay.

To Mobile Bay we're bound away,
A-screwing cotton by the day.

Up aloft this yard must go,
Let the wind blow high or low.

Blow away bullies, blow away men;
Blow away bullies; we'll try him again.

I wish I was in Boston town,
...nking good stiff Boston gin.

...the sails they shine;
...ling the line.

Captain Edward B. Trumbull

To Mobile Bay we're bound away,
> Wa-a-ay, blow the man down!
A-screwing cotton by the day,
> Give us some time to blow the man down!

Up aloft this yard must go,
> Wa-a-ay, blow the man down!
Let the wind blow high and low,
> Give us some time to blow the man down!

Blow away bullies, blow away men,
> Wa-a-ay, blow the man down!
Blow away bullies; we'll try him again,
> Give us some time to blow the man down!

I wish I was in Boston town,
> Wa-a-ay, blow the man down!
A-drinking good stiff Boston gin,
> Give us some time to blow the man down!

The wind is fair; the sails they shine,
> Wa-a-ay, blow the man down!
The Boston girls are pulling the line,
> Give us some time to blow the man down!

TRADITIONAL – 1868 - 1874

Blow the Man Down, courtesy of The James Madison Carpenter collection (AFC 1972/001), American Folklife Center, Library of Congress, Washington, D.C.

Santa Anna

Captain Trumbull gave Carpenter only two verses of this song, *Santa Anna*.[13] Perhaps it was all that he could remember at the time.

Santa Anna, as I've heard say,
Hurrah, Santa Anna!
He lost his leg, then ran away;
Along the plains of Mexico!

He was a man of widest fame,
Hurrah, Santa Anna!
And that is how he gained his name;
Along the plains of Mexico!

TRADITIONAL – 1868

Old Horse

Old Horse[14] given to Carpenter by Captain Trumbull in 1927 and is similar to the version Eckstrom included in *Minstrelsy of Maine: Folk-Songs and Ballads of the Woods and the Coast*.[15] Eckstrom feels that it is a Maine song because of its mention of Saccarap' (or Saccarappa – now Westbrook, Maine) and Portland, Maine and its industrial connection between the two towns. Paving blocks were cut in Saccarappa and hauled by horses to Portland to be loaded on to sailing vessels.[16] The song could be much older since sailors throughout history have always complained about their food on ship.

Old Horse! Old Horse!
How came you here?

"I've carted stones for many a year,
From Sacarac to Portland Pier.

And after long and sore abuse,
I'm salted down for sailor's use.

The sailors they do me despise;
They turn me over and damn my eyes.

They out the flesh from my bones,
They throw the rest to Davy Jones.

TRADITIONAL – 1868 - 1874

One More Day

Carpenter wrote down *One More Day* [17] in 1927 from the singing of Captain Edward B. Trumbull.

Only one more day, my darling;
One more day;
Only one more day, my darling;
Only one more day!

We land in dock tomorrow
One more day;
Soon our worries will be over;
Only one more day!

We'll furl our sails and make her fast;
Only one more day;
This homeward voyage will be our last;
Only one more day!

TRADITIONAL – 1868 - 1874

Bound for the Rio Grande

Bound for the Rio Grande[18] learned circa 1868 by Trumbull Captain of the *Braque Taria Topan*. The *Taria Topan's* homeport was Salem and the ship just completed one of the fastest passages from Zanzibar to Boston.

We're bound away this very day,
    Away, Rio!
We're bound away this very day,
    For we're bound for the Rio Grande!

    Then away, Rio!
    Away Rio!
    Sing fare you well, my bonnie young gal,
    For we're bound for the Rio Grande!

So heave her up and let her go,
    Away, Rio!
So heave her up and let her go,
    For we're bound for the Rio Grande!

    Then away, Rio!
    Away Rio!
    Sing fare you well, my bonnie young gal,
    For we're bound for the Rio Grande!

We are leaving the pretty young girls in the town,
    Away, Rio!
And when we come back we will bring a silk gown.
    For we're bound for the Rio Grande!

Then away, Rio!
   Away Rio!
Sing fare you well, my bonnie young gal,
   For we're bound for the Rio Grande!

We have a good ship and a good steady crew;
   Away, Rio!
A knock down mate and a hard skipper too.
   For we're bound for the Rio Grande!

Then away, Rio!
   Away Rio!
Sing fare you well, my bonnie young gal,
   For we're bound for the Rio Grande!

TRADITIONAL – 1868 - 1874

Taria Topan Postcard, courtesy of Sal Pangallo

Ruben Ranzo

Ruben Ranzo [19] was part of the Carpenter Collection with credit given to Captain Trumbull but no additional notes or dates were listed. In Trumbull's version, after the sailor is whipped for not doing his duties, the Captain took him in and gave him brandy. The sailor then courts the Captain's daughter. Gladly, his whaling days are now over.

Ruben Ranzo was sung when the Marine Society of Salem, Massachusetts celebrated the one hundred and fiftieth anniversary of the club's existence on October 27, 1921. The format of the meeting proceeded with words from the honored guest Captain James Gurney, President of the Boston Marine Society. The celebration continued with a six-course dinner beginning with oysters on the half shell and ending with coffee, cheroots, and stogies. As the courses were being served, various nautical terms were explained to the "landlubbers," with ample time taken to sing *Ruben Ranzo, Whiskey Johnny, Sally Brown* and other "rollicking sea songs" led by the Master, Captain Edward B. Trumbull. "The choruses were heartily responded by all." [20] Trumbull, master and treasurer of the society then concluded, "much as we would desire to prolong the gaiety, the end must come at last and the hour to 'turn in' was approaching" [20]

Captain Edward B. Trumbull's home at 90 Federal Street Salem, courtesy of Mary Barker

Oh Ranzo was no sailor,
Ranzo, boys! Ranzo!
He shipped on board of a whaler,
Ranzo, boys! Ranzo!

Oh Ranzo was no sailor,
Ranzo, boys! Ranzo!
He was a Germen tailor,
Ranzo, boys! Ranzo!

He could not do his duty,
Ranzo, boys! Ranzo!
It seemed to him a pity.
Ranzo, boys! Ranzo!

They gave him four and twenty,
Ranzo, boys! Ranzo!
Which was nineteen More than plenty.
Ranzo, boys! Ranzo!

The captain being a good man,
Ranzo, boys! Ranzo!
He took him to the cabin.
Ranzo, boys! Ranzo!

He gave him rum and brandy,
Ranzo, boys! Ranzo!
He always kept it handy.
Ranzo, boys! Ranzo!

He courted the captain's daughter,
Ranzo, boys! Ranzo!
No more will a ship on a whaler.
Ranzo, boys! Ranzo!

TRADITIONAL – 1868 - 1874

The Wide Missouri

Shenandoah is still a favorite melody sung today and loved by many. Captain Edward B. Trumbull of Salem collected *The Wide Missouri*[21] in 1870. Similar versions of *Shenandoah* can be found in numerous folk collections and our collective conscience.

Oh Shenandoah, I love your daughter;
    Hurray! Away, you rolling river!
Oh Shenandoah, I love you daughter;
    Ah-ha, I'm bound away, on the wide Missouri!

The Missouri is a mighty river;
    Hurray! Away, you rolling river!
I love the place where runs her water.
    Ah-ha, I'm bound away, on the wide Missouri!

Oh, Shenandoah, I'm going to leave you;
    Hurray! Away, you rolling river!
Oh, Shenandoah, won't you be sorry!
    Ah-ha, I'm bound away, on the wide Missouri!

Oh, Shenandoah, I long to hear you;
    Hurray! Away, you rolling river!
Oh, Shenandoah, I'll ne'er forget you!
    Ah-ha, I'm bound away, on the wide Missouri!

We're bound away this very day, sir;
    Hurray! Away, you rolling river!
Heave her up and let her go, sir!
    Ah-ha, I'm bound away, on the wide Missouri!

Captain Edward B. Trumbull

We're going to-day to cross the water;
    Hurray! Away, you rolling river!
We'll carry with us the old-side-wheeler.
    Ah-ha, I'm bound away, on the wide Missouri!

We're sailing down the Mississippi;
    Hurray! Away, you rolling river!
We're going out by Eads Jetty.
    Ah-ha, I'm bound away, on the wide Missouri!

TRADITIONAL – 1870

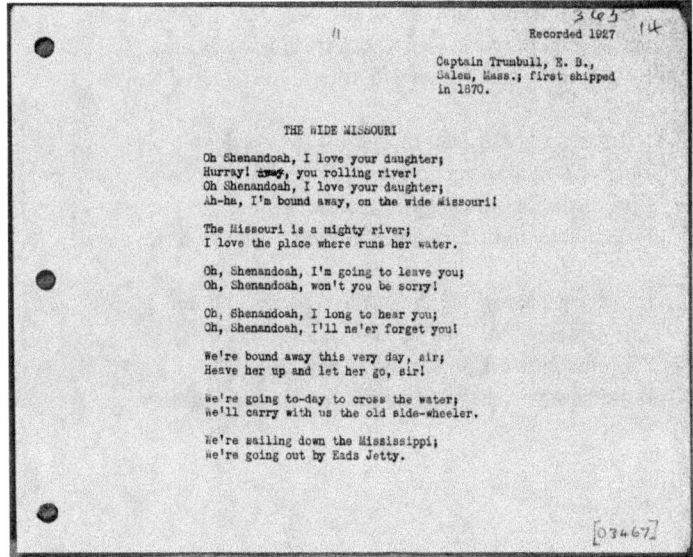

The Wide Missouri, courtesy of The James Madison Carpenter collection (AFC 1972/001), American Folklife Center, Library of Congress, Washington, D.C.

The Dreadnaught

Carpenter wrote down this version of *The Dreadnaught*[22] in 1927 from the recitation of Captain Edward B. Trumbull from Salem. The *Dreadnaught* was a clipper ship built in 1853 in Newburyport, Massachusetts. This ship is considered "a Liverpool packet" because she traded with Liverpool, England and was not build there.[23] She made extremely fast passages crossing the Atlantic between New York and Liverpool for the Red Cross Line. The ship went down while rounding Cape Horn in 1869.[24]

It's a fine packet, a packet of fame;
She's a Liverpool packet, and the Dreadnaught's her name;
She sails to the westward where stormy winds blow;
Bound away to the westward in the Dreadnaught we go.

It's now we are hauling through Waterloo dock;
The boys and the girls on the pier-head to flock;
With three loud cheers as the tears do flow;
Bound away to the westward in the Dreadnaught we go.

It's now we are sailing down the wild Irish shore;
The passengers all sick and the sailors all sore;
The crew on deck all around to and fro;
Bound away to the westward in the Dreadnaught we go.

Captain Edward B. Trumbull

Its now we are sailing over the ocean so blue;
Our officers an deck, also our crew;
The sails all set aloft and below;
Bound away to the westward in the Dreadnaught we go.

Its now we are sailing down the Long Island shore;
The pilot he boards us as he has often done before;
Fill away the main-topsl, and let her go by;
She's the Liverpool packet, Lord God let her fly!

Three cheers for Captain Samuels and his bully crew,
Three cheers from the Dreadnaught where're she may go,
This song was composed in the Starboard watch below;
God bless the Old Dreadnaught where're she may go!

TRADITIONAL – 1868 - 1874

Captain Edward B. Trumbull's obituary transcribed from the *Boston Post* dated October 31, 1934, Part I:

> Captain Edward B. Trumbull, prominent seafarer and public spirited citizen, passed away this morning at the Salem Hospital in the 82^{sd} year. He was one of the few remaining merchant marines of Salem and during his life he sailed to practically every recognized port in the world, spreading the fame of Salem and her maritime glory. His home, 90 Federal Street, was a treasure house of relics and curios, gathered during his many trips. [25]

Blow, Boys, Blow!

This version of *Blow, Boys, Blow!* [26] was written down in 1927 by Carpenter from the recitation of Captain Edward B. Trumbull from Salem. Verse three was omitted because racial biased language.

> Yankee ships come down the river;
> Blow, Boys, Blow!
> Her masts and yards they shine like silver!
> Blow, my bullyboys, blow!

> How d'ye know she's a Yankee ship, sir?
> Blow, Boys, Blow!
> By the stars and stripes that fly above her.
> Blow, my bullyboys, blow!

> What d'ye suppose they have for dinner?
> Blow, Boys, Blow!
> Sawdust and bullock's liver.
> Blow, my bullyboys, blow!

> Where d'ye suppose the ship is bound for?
> Blow, Boys, Blow!
> She's bound away for London town, sir!
> Blow, my bullyboys, blow!

> All the girls are on the pier head,
> Blow, Boys, Blow!
> Wiping their eyes for lots of sorrow.
> Blow, my bullyboys, blow!

> Up loft this yard must go,
> > Blow, Boys, Blow!
> Let the wind blow high or low.
> > Blow, my bullyboys, blow!

TRADITIONAL – 1868

Captain Edward B. Trumbull's obituary transcribed from the *Boston Post* dated October 31, 1934, Part II:

> Captain Trumbull was born in Salem, April 28, 1853, the son of the late Captain Edward H. and Mrs. Mary Ann (Ashby) Trumbull. His father was a shipmaster who made voyages to various ports of the world. After graduating from the Phillips school, the son became a clerk in a Salem store, but not liking it, and being possessed of the desire to go to sea, like Salem boys of that period, he secured a chance to go in the ship Mutlah, Captain Otis Ballad, and sailed from Boston, August 1, 1868, and made port, and made a round voyage between that port, Hong Kong, Manila and return to Boston.
>
> His next voyage was in the ship Formosa, to Melbourne, Australia, Newcastle, N. S. W., Hong Kong, Manila and back to Boston. Captain Charles H. Allen, Jr., was the master, and the vessel was owned by Stone, Silsbee, Pickman & Allen of Salem, A second voyage was made in the same ship. On the passage home the vessel was struck in Gasper Straits, and was obliged to go to Batavia for repairs, where she remained for five months. [27]

Hoodah Day Shanty

Captain Trumbull's version of the *Hoodah Day Shanty*[8] was collected in 1868 and transcribed by Carpenter in 1927 for his thesis. The melody, *Camptown Races* written by Stephen Foster was used in numerous versions of this song as the song progressed and changed over the years. Refer to the section, *Off to California:*

>The California Gold Diggers
>Ho! Boys Ho!
>The Californian
>The Hoodah Day Shanty
>Banks of the Sacramento

Carpenter writes in his thesis about *On the Banks of the Sacramento*, "The shanty has the same tune and chorus as Wood's Minstrel song, *Gwine to Run all Night*. It is practically impossible to determine which is copy, for it is noted that the chantey never used any of the regular verses of the minstrel." [28] Carpenter collected two versions of the *Hoodah Day Shanty*, one from England, and Trumbull's American version.

>As I was a walking down Liverpool Street,
>   A Hoo-dah, and A hoo-dah!
>I met a young girl who was pretty and sweet,
>   And A Hoo-dah, hoo-dah-day!

>>Chorus: Blow, boys, blow,
>>   For California O,
>>   There's plenty of gold, so I've been told,
>>   On the banks of the Sacramento.

Captain Edward B. Trumbull

Her-waist-was-small, her eyes were grey
    A Hoo-dah, and A hoo-dah!
She looked at me, then turned away.
    And A Hoo-dah, hoo-dah-day!

    Chorus: Blow, boys, blow,
        For California O,
        There's plenty of gold, so I've been told,
        On the banks of the Sacramento.

I asked her if she'd come aboard,
    A Hoo-dah, and A hoo-dah!
She said she would not break her word;
    And A Hoo-dah, hoo-dah-day!

    Chorus: Blow, boys, blow,
        For California O,
        There's plenty of gold, so I've been told,
        On the banks of the Sacramento.

For she had a sailor out at sea,
    A Hoo-dah, and A hoo-dah!
And she wouldn't leave him now for me!
    And A Hoo-dah, hoo-dah-day!

    Chorus: Blow, boys, blow,
        For California O,
        There's plenty of gold, so I've been told,
        On the banks of the Sacramento.

TRADITIONAL – 1868

Hoodah Day Shanty, courtesy of The James Madison Carpenter collection (AFC 1972/001), American Folklife Center, Library of Congress, Washington, D.C.

Whisky Johnny

Carpenter recorded *Whisky Johnny*, a hoisting chantey in 1927 from Captain Edward B. Trumbull while he was on the *Bark Taria Topan*, first shipped 1868.[29] Carpenter wrote in an article from the *New York Times* called *Lusty Chanteys From Dead Ships of Sail* "if not for the sea, what, according to their records, was the uppermost in their (sailor's) minds?"[30] In *Whisky Johnny* it becomes obvious.

>Whisky is the life of man,
>Whisky, Johnny!
>I drink whiskey while I can,
>Whisky for my Johnny!
>
>I wish I had some whisky now,
>Whisky, Johnny!
>I'd tip her up and down she'd go,
>Whisky for my Johnny!
>
>Whisky killed my poor old man,
>Whisky, Johnny!
>Whisky from a rusty can,
>Whisky for my Johnny!
>
>Whisky made my mammy cry,
>Whisky, Johnny!
>Whisky made the boson sigh,
>Whisky for my Johnny!
>
>Whisky kills the whole ship's crew,
>Whisky, Johnny!
>I hope whisky kills me too,
>Whisky for my Johnny!

Captain Edward B. Trumbull

I thought I heard the old man say,
Whisky, Johnny!
One more heave and then belay,
Whisky for my Johnny!

Up aloft this yard must go,
Whisky, Johnny!
Let the wind blow high or low,
Whisky for my Johnny!

We're bound away this very day,
Whisky, Johnny!
We're bound away for Mobile Bay,
Whisky for my Johnny!

We're bound away to Mobile Bay,
Whisky, Johnny!
A screwing cotton by the day,
Whisky for my Johnny!

TRADITIONAL – 1868

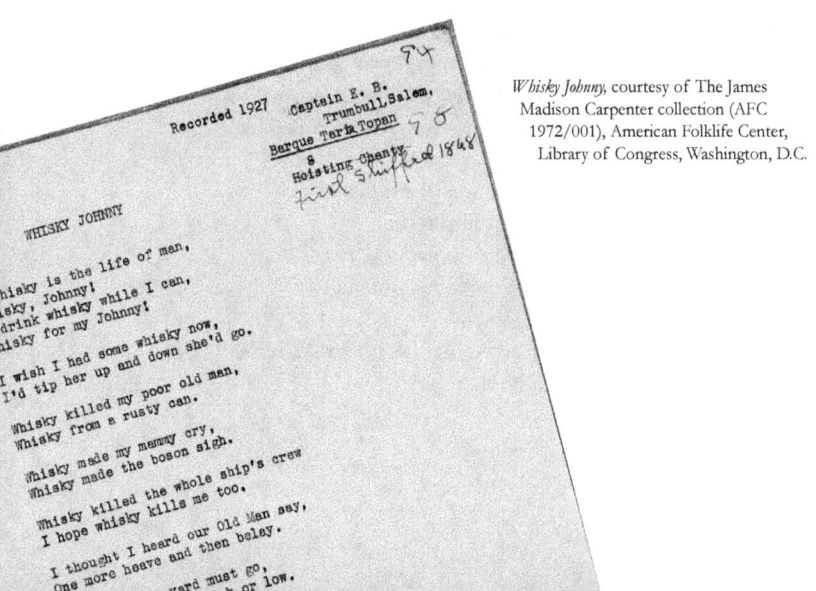

Whisky Johnny, courtesy of The James Madison Carpenter collection (AFC 1972/001), American Folklife Center, Library of Congress, Washington, D.C.

My Own Country

Carpenter got this version of *My Own Country* [31] from Captain Edward B. Trumbull in 1927. This song is also known as *Home Boys Home* and sometime called *Bell Bottom Trousers* or *The Servant of Rosemary Lane*. [32] Several of these versions have various endings, giving warning to "young maids."

> So come all you young maidens, a warning take by me,
> Never trust a sailor lad an inch above your knee,
> For I trusted one and he beguiled me,
> And left me with a pair o' twins to dangle on me knee.

Trumbull's version of *My Own Country* gives the maiden not only gold, but hope that the sailor will return home in the spring.

When first I went to service in Salisbury Lane,
I gained the good will of my master and dame,
When a young sailor he came there for to stay,
And that was the beginning of my first misery.

Chorus: Oh it's home, dearest home! It's home I'd like to be!
        It's home, dearest home in my own country,
        Where the oak and the ash and the bonny willow tree,
        Are all growing green in sweet North Amerikee!

The sailor growing sleepy, he hung down his head,
And asked for a candle to light him to be.
I lit him to bed, as a maid ought to do,
And he smiled as he said, "Won't you come in too?"

Chorus: Oh it's home, dearest home! It's home I'd like to be!
        It's home, dearest home in my own country,

Where the oak and the ash and the bonny willow tree,
Are all growing green in sweet North Amerikee!

I jumped in beside him to keep his back warm,
Thinking the sailor would do me no harm;
But the night it was cold, and the sailor he grew bold,
And what was done that night I dare not unfold.

Chorus: Oh it's home, dearest home! It's home I'd like to be!
    It's home, dearest home in my own country,
    Where the oak and the ash and the bonny willow tree,
    Are all growing green in sweet North Amerikee!

Early next morning the sailor he arose,
And into my apron threw hands full of gold;
The gold it did glisten and it dazzled of my eyes,
"Come, marry me, my fair maid!" the sailor he cries.

Chorus: Oh it's home, dearest home! It's home I'd like to be!
    It's home, dearest home in my own country,
    Where the oak and the ash and the bonny willow tree,
    Are all growing green in sweet North Amerikee!

"When the babe is born, you can put it out to nurse;
Maintain it with the gold that you have in the purse.
Wrap it up warm and keep it till next spring,
And that is the time that I will return again.

Chorus: Oh it's home, dearest home! It's home I'd like to be!
    It's home, dearest home in my own country,
    Where the oak and the ash and the bonny willow tree,
    Are all growing green in sweet North Amerikee!

TRADITIONAL – 1868

Haul The Bowline

Carpenter states that the song *Haul The Bowline*[33] is a short, pull shanty. Carpenter recorded the song for his thesis in 1927 from Captain Edward B. Trumbull of Salem. Trumbull learned the chantey circa 1868 from one of his crew. Poet John Masefield wrote in his book, *A Sailor's Garland*, "Of the sheet, tack and bowline shanties the oldest is *Haul The Bowline,* which was certainly in use in the reign of Henry VIII. It is still very popular, though the bowline is no longer the rope it was." [34]

> Haul the bowline, the main to gallant bowline;
> Haul the bowline, the bowline haul!
>
> Haul the bowline, Sally is me darling;
> Haul the bowline, the bowline haul!
>
> Haul the bowline, the ship (packet) she is rollin';
> Haul the bowline, the bowline haul!
>
> Heave, heave and haul her; we'll either strain or break her;
> Haul the bowline, the bowline haul!
>
> Haul the bowline, the captain is a growlin';
> Haul the bowline, the bowline haul!
>
> Haul the bowline, get up in the mornin';
> Haul the bowline, the bowline haul!

TRADITIONAL – 1868

Captain Edward B. Trumbull's obituary transcribed from the *Boston Post* dated October 31, 1934, Part III:

> He next sailed two voyages as second mate and a voyage as mate on the barque Glide and 16 voyages on the barque Taria Topin, nine as mate and seven as master, when he retired from sea in 1890. He was the sole survivor of the officers of the last named vessel. A coincidence is that as a boy he was on the Taria Topin when she was launched in 1870. He estimated that he had sailed about 500,00 miles during his sea life. He was manager of the Salem Storage warehouse since it was built.
>
> He married Miss Lizzie F, daughter of the late Daniel A. and Elizabeth R. Manning, who died a few years ago. He leaves one sister, Mrs. Joseph Abbott of Salem, and a grandson, Edward Trumbull Batchelder.
>
> He joined Starr King Lodge, A. F. and A. M. in 1880. He was at one time a member of the license commission of Salem, and its chairman and he also declines being a candidate for mayor. For several years he was master of the Salem Marine Society of Salem. [36]

Pete Seeger performing at the Salem Maritime Festival on Derby Wharf 1990, with Daisy Nell and Bill and Sarah Smith, courtesy of Jim McAllister

Acknowledgments

When I began compiling material my first book *Old Salem in Ballad and Song*, I found several songs with a link to Salem's maritime past. Since then, I have collected over 200 songs, ballads, and tunes, I decided to separate *Old Salem in Ballad and Song* into a two book series with the second one being called *Old Salem at Sea in Ballad and Song* Series II. I have included 89 sea songs, ballads, and sea shanties in this book that all have a relationship to Salem and to the sea. I have also included endnotes and references.

I would like to thank my wife Jennifer for her support throughout this process, for her work at the Salem Public Library, and for developing the website, Salem Links and Lore, a local source for Salem history, found on the Salem Public Library's website. I am particularity thankful to Bill and Sarah Smith, longtime friends, Salem residents and folk musicians, for their continual support and encouragement with this project. Thank you to local folk singer, songwriter, and schooner skipper Daisy Nell, for writing the foreword and for sharing her music. Special thanks to Sal Pangallo, Betsey and Ed Bennett, Jim Dalton, and Christine Elizabeth Mistretta for the use of their private collections. Thank you, Darleen Melis for help with editing, maritime photographer Mary Barker for the use of her photographs of Salem, artist Glenn Church, and to my daughter, Rosie Strom for sharing her graphic design knowledge, suggestions, and talent.

I would also like to thank all the librarians for their knowledge and support at the following libraries: Boston Public Library, California State Library, Center for Popular Music, Middle Tennessee State University, David M. Rubenstein Rare Book & Manuscript Library at Duke University, Flanders Collection at Middlebury College, Middlebury Vermont, Frederick E. Berry Library at Salem State University, Historic Beverly, Lester S. Levy Collection of Sheet Music, at Johns Hopkins University, Library of Congress, Philips

Library at the Peabody Essex Museum in Rowley and Salem, Providence Public Library, Salem Marine Society, Salem Public Library, Tabernacle Church's Historic Room in Salem, and the Vaughan Williams Memorial Library at the Cecil Sharp House in London.

Lastly, I would like to acknowledge all our music friends and local sessions for which we all share our love of music and community.

Enjoy Salem and keep singing - Bob Strom

Nautical photographer, **Mary Barker** specializes in candid environmental photography, documenting the restoration of the historic wooden fishing vessels, as well as capturing schooners and other tall ships both dockside and under sail. Mary is the resident documentarian for the *Schooner Adventure* and considered "one of our own" at Gloucester Marine Railways. Mary's nautical restoration photographs have been featured in *Wooden Boat*, *Marlinspike*, *Sea History Magazine,* and the *2018 Tall Ship Directory.*

Endnotes

INTRODUCTION

1. Journal of a Voyage Barque *San Francisco* 1849 - 1850, Captain Thomas Remmonds - on display at the Historic Beverly, Beverly Massachusetts & Around the Horn, retrieved online October 5, 2018, http://www.larcomfamilytree.com/around-the-horn/.
2. Gale Huntington, *Songs the Whalemen Sang* (New York: Barre Publishing Company, Dover Publications, Inc., 1970, First Printed 1964), 68 & Stuart M. Frank, *Songs of the Sea and Shore*, Folkways Records FH 5256, New York, 1980, LP.
3. Gale Huntington, *The Gam, More Songs the Whalemen Sang* (Northfield, MN: Loomis Press, 2014).
4. Mark Alan Lovewell, *Singing Their Stories, Sailor Chanties Are Musical Memories, Vineyard Gazette*, Wednesday, July 30, 2014.
5. Larry Kaplan, *Song for Gale, Worth All the Telling*, a Folk-Legacy recording, CD 122, Sharon CT, 1988, CD.
6. Gale Huntington, *Songs the Whalemen Sang* (New York: Barre Publishing Company, Dover Publications, Inc., 1970, First Printed 1964), 209 - 210.
7. Frederick Pease Harlow, *The Making of a Sailor or Sea Life Aboard a Yankee Square-Rigger* (Salem, Massachusetts: Marine Research Society of Salem, Massachusetts, 1928).
8. Frederick Pease Harlow, *Chanteying Aboard American Ships* (Barre, Mass.: Barre Press, 1962).
9. Gertrude Gilleland Harlow, Harlow Family Papers, Biographical Sketch 1829 - 1962, The Collections Research Center (CRC) at Mystic Seaport, retrieved online October 25, 2108, https://research.mysticseaport.org/coll/coll287/#head50670896.
10. Frederick Pease Harlow, *Chanteying Aboard American Ships* (Barre, Mass.: Barre Press, 1962), 32.
11. Stan Hugill, *Shanties From the Seven Seas* (Mystic, CT: Mystic Seaport, 2003, Original Publisher, Routledge & Kegan Paul, Inc. 1961), 151.
12. Frederick Pease Harlow, *The Making of a Sailor or Sea Life Aboard a Yankee Square-Rigger* (Salem, Massachusetts: Marine Research Society of Salem, Massachusetts, 1928), 219.
13. Stan Hugill, *Shanties From the Seven Seas* (Mystic, CT: Mystic Seaport, 2003. Original Publisher, Routledge & Kegan Paul, Inc. 1961), 50, 110.
14. William Main Doerflinger, *Songs of the Sailor and Lumberman* (Glennwood, Illinois: Meyerbooks, 3rd Edition, 1990), 322.

15. Stan Hugill, *Shanties From the Seven Seas* (Mystic, CT: Mystic Seaport, 2003, Original Publisher, Routledge & Kegan Paul, Inc. 1961), 277 & Frederick Pease Harlow, *The Making of a Sailor or Sea Life Aboard a Yankee Square-Rigger* (Salem, Massachusetts: Marine Research Society of Salem, Massachusetts, 1928), 124.
16. A Noble Company, Box 18, Folder 1, MSS 74, Silsbee Family Papers, Phillips Library, Peabody Essex Museum, Rowley, MA

I. OFF TO CALIFORNIA

I Come From Salem City
1. Stephen Foster, *Oh Susanna* (New York: C., Holt, Jr., 1848).
2. Library of Congress, Stephen Foster, retrieved online December 20, 2018 https://www.loc.gov/item/ihas.200035701.
3. Alfred Peabody, "On The Early Days and Rapid Growth of California," *Essex Institute Historical Collection vol. 12 - 13* (Salem, Massachusetts: Essex Institute, The Salem Press, 1872), 106.
4. Ralph D. Paine, *The Ships and Sailors of Old Salem* (New York: The Outing Publishing Company, 1908), 648.
5. Frank Shay, *American Sailor's Treasury: Sea Chanteys, Legends and Lore* (New York: Smithmark Publishers, Inc., 1991), 120.
6. Journal of a Voyage Barque *San Francisco*, Captain Thomas Remmonds - on display at the Beverly Historical Society, Beverly, Massachusetts.

The California Gold Diggers
7. Jesse Hutchison, Jr., N. Emmett, *The California Gold Diggers* (Philadelphia: E.L. Walker, 1849) retrieved online July 16, 2019, https://levysheetmusic.mse.jhu.edu/collection/018/040.
8. Irwin Silber, *Songs of the Great American West* (New York: The Macmillan Company, 1967), 9.
9. Bark *La Grange* logbook, log 621, Passenger Journal, Phillips Library, Peabody Essex Museum, Rowley, MA
10. Bark *La Grange* logbook, Log 1001, Phillips Library, Peabody Essex Museum, Rowley, MA
11. Lowell Mason, *Carmina Sacra*: or, *Boston Collection of Church Music: comprising the most popular psalm and hymn tunes in eternal use together with a great variety of new tunes, chants, sentences, motetts* (Boston: J. H. Wilkins & R. B. Carter, 1841).
12. Bark *La Grange* logbook, Log 1702, Phillips Library, Peabody Essex Museum, Rowley, MA

13. Stephen Foster, *Camptown Races* (New York: C., Holt, Jr., 1848).
14. William Main Doerflinger, *Songs of the Sailor and Lumberman* (Glennwood, Illinois: Meyerbooks, 3rd Edition, 1990), 67.

I've Been Dreamin'

15. Bill Adams, Robert Frothingham, ed., *I've Been Dreamin'* in *Songs of the Sea and Sailors' Chanteys* (Cambridge: Houghton Mifflin Co. The Riverside Press, 1924), 13.

Witch of the Wave

16. Arthur H. Clark, *The Clipper Ship Era, 1843 - 1869* (New York and London: G. P. Putnam's Sons, 1911), 166.
17. Vertical File in Salem Collection - Bertram, John & Salem Links and Lore, retrieved online October 10, 2018, http://www.noblenet.org/salem/wiki/index.php/Bertram,_John.

Witch of the Wave (tune)

18. Ralph Sweet, ed., *The Fifer's Delight* (Enfield CT: 1981 Originally Published 1966), 63 & Patrick Sky, ed., *Ryan's Mammoth Collection of Fiddle Tunes, 1050 Reels and Jigs* (Pacific, MO: Mel Bay, 1965, Originally Published (Boston, Massachusetts: Publisher Elias Howe, 1883), 24.

Gold

19. Bark *La Grange* logbook, Log 1702, Phillips Library, Peabody Essex Museum, Rowley, MA

The Gold Hunter's Story

20. Bark *La Grange* logbook, Log 1702, Phillips Library, Peabody Essex Museum, Rowley, MA

The Returned Californian

21. James Pierpont and John P Ordway, *The Returned Californian* (Boston: E. H. Wade, monographic, 1852). retrieved online December 19, 2018, https://www.loc.gov/item/sm1852.501530/.
22. Wikipedia contributors, "James Lord Pierpont," Wikipedia, The Free Encyclopedia, retrieved online January 31, 2019, https://en.wikipedia.org/wiki/James_Lord_Pierpont.

II. SUPERSTITION

The Mermaid
1. Francis James Childs, *English and Scottish Popular Ballads*, Helen Child Sargent and George Lyman Kittredge, ed. (Boston and New York: Houghton Mifflin Company, Cambridge: The Riverside Press, 1904), 615.
2. William Chappell, *Popular Music of the Olden Time* vol. II (New York: Dover Publication, Inc., 1965), 742.
3. Paul Clayton, *Whaling And Sailing Songs, From the Days of Moby Dick*, Tradition Records, TLP 1005, 1956, LP & David Jones, *Widdecombe Fair*, Festival Five Records, 2003, CD.
4. Bertrand Harris, *The Traditional Tunes of the Child Ballads, vol. 4, with Their Texts* (Princeton, New Jersey: Princeton University Press, 1972), 370.

Of The Lost Ship
5. Eugene Richard White, Robert Frothingham, ed., *I've Been Dreamin'* in *Songs of the Sea and Sailors' Chanteys* (Cambridge: Houghton Mifflin Co., The Riverside Press, 1924), 183 & Eugene Richard White, *Songs for Good Fighting*, (Vigo Street, London: Elkin Mathews, 1908), 10.

The Gosport Tragedy or The Ship's Carpenter
6. Ship *Vaughan* logbook, Log 1057, Phillips Library, Peabody Essex Museum, Rowley, MA
7. Robert B. Waltz & David G. Engle, "The Ballad Index," *The Cruel Ship's Carpenter, The Gosport Tragedy, Pretty Polly* (Laws P36A/B), retrieved online June 24, 2019, https://www.fresnostate.edu/folklore/ballads/LP36.html.
8. Edith Fowke, *The Penguin Book of Canadian Folk Songs* (Canada: Markham, Penguin Books, 1986), 162.
9. Ralph Delahaye Paine, *The Ships and Sailors of Old Salem: The Record of a Brilliant Era of American Achievement* (Chicago: C. McClurg & Co., 1912), 36 & Gale Huntington, *Songs the Whalemen Sang* (New York: Barre Publishing Company, Dover Publications, Inc., 1970, First Printed 1964), 129.

III. SALEM SHIP'S and PRISONS LOG BOOKS

Hills of Georgetown
1. Bark *La Grange* logbook, Log 1702, Phillips Library, Peabody Essex Museum, Rowley, MA

Lines composed on a court martial of Oliver Poland on board The America
2. Ship *America* logbook, Log 918, Phillips Library, Peabody Essex Museum, Rowley, MA

The Sailor's Early Home
3. Bark *La Grange* Passenger Journal, Log 621, Phillips Library, Peabody Essex Museum, Rowley, MA
4. Charles Walton Sanders, *Union Fifth Reader, Embracing a Full Exposition of the Principles of Rhetorical Reading* (New York and Chicago: Ivison, Blakeman, Taylor & Co. Publishers, 1876), 359.

Of Dartmore Prison
5. *Journal of Joseph Valpey, Jr., of Salem*, November, 1813 - April, 1815, with other papers relating to his experience in Dartmoor prison (Detroit, Michigan: Michigan Society of Colonial Wars, Burton Historical Collection, Detroit Public Library, 1922), 1.
6. Wikipedia contributors: HM Prison Dartmoor, Wikipedia, The Free Encyclopedia, retrieved online October 9, 2018, https://en.wikipedia.org/wiki/HM_Prison_Dartmoor.

Hunting for Lice and Fleas
7. *Journal of Joseph Valpey, Jr., of Salem*, November, 1813 - April, 1815, with other papers relating to his experience in Dartmoor prison (Detroit, Michigan: Michigan Society of Colonial Wars, Burton Historical Collection, Detroit Public Library, 1922), 34.

The Fruits of Gambling's
8. Wikipedia contributors: *HM Prison Dartmoor*, Wikipedia, The Free Encyclopedia, retrieved online October 9, 2018, https://en.wikipedia.org/wiki/HM_Prison_Dartmoor.

9. *Journal of Joseph Valpey, Jr., of Salem*, November, 1813 - April, 1815, with other papers relating to his experience in Dartmoor Prison (Detroit, Michigan: Michigan Society of Colonial Wars, Burton Historical Collection, Detroit Public Library, 1922), 33.

Ship Bengal at Sea
10. Ship *Bengal* logbook, Log 302, Phillips Library, Peabody Essex Museum, Rowley, MA

The Greenland Whale
11. Ship *Bengal* logbook, Log 302, Phillips Library, Peabody Essex Museum, Rowley, MA
12. Gale Huntington, *Songs the Whalemen Sang* (New York: Barre Publishing Company, Dover Publications, Inc., 1970, First Printed 1964), 11.
13. Starboard List, *Songs of the Tall Ships* & *Cruising 'Round Yarmouth*, Genes Records, GCD 1025/27, 1996, CD.

The Sea Ran High
14. Gale Huntington, *Songs the Whalemen Sang* (New York: Barre Publishing Company, Dover Publications, Inc., 1970, First Printed 1964), 81.
15. Larry Kaplan, *Furthermore,* Hannah Lane Music, 2016, CD.
16. *The Sailor's Magazine and Naval Journal, vol. 5* (New York: American Seamen's Friend Society, Published by American Seamen's Friend Society, George P. Scott & Co. 1833), 248.

The Captain Calls All Hands
17. Gale Huntington, *Songs the Whalemen Sang* (New York: Barre Publishing Company, Dover Publications, Inc., 1970, First Printed 1964), 99.
18. Stuart M. Frank, *Songs of the Sea and Shore,* Folkways Records FH 5256, New York, 1980, LP.
19. Stuart M. Frank, *Jolly Sailors Bold Ballads and Songs of the American Sailor* (East Windsor, New Jersey: Camsco Music, 2010), 51.

Sharply Its Breath the Vessel Feels
20. Ship *George* logbook, Log 291, Phillips Library, Peabody Essex Museum, Rowley, MA

Blow! Oh Blow!
21. Bark *Borneo* logbook, Log 983, Phillips Library, Peabody Essex Museum, Rowley, MA

Merrily, Merrily
22. Bark *Borneo* logbook, Log 983, Phillips Library, Peabody Essex Museum, Rowley, MA
23. J. W. Lake, *The Poetical Works of Sir Walter Scott: With a Sketch of His Life By Sir Walter Scott* (Philadelphia: J Crissy No 4 Minor Street and Thomas Cowperthwait & Co., No 263 Market Street, 1838), 268.

The Wandering Sailor

24. Ship *Astrea* logbook, Log 11, Phillips Library, Peabody Essex Museum, Rowley, MA & William Drysdale, *The Princess of Montserrat: Strange Narrative of Adventure and Peril on Land and Sea* (Albany, NY: Albany Book Company, 1890), 168.

The Faithful Sailor

25. Ship *Astrea* logbook, Log 11, Phillips Library, Peabody Essex Museum, Rowley, MA
26. *The Sailor's Farewell,* together with *The Sailor's Return,* and *The Praise of Women,* Isaiah Thomas Broadside Ballads Project, retrieved online, October 13, 2018, http://www.americanantiquarian.org/thomasballads/items/show/214.

IV. LIFE AT SEA

Home Again

1. *Home Again* from Kenneth S. Goldstein Collection of American Song Broadsides Center for Popular Music, Middle Tennessee State University, retrieved online July 18, 2017, http://popmusic. mtsu.edu. & Marshall S. Pike, *Home Again* (Salem, Massachusetts: J. Peckman) 1858.

The Seaman

2. "The Seaman," *Salem Gazette,* August 2, 1811, #2092.

The Sailor's Watch At Sea

3. "The Sailor's Watch At Sea," *Salem Gazette,* January 25, 1820.

A Sailor's Life

4. "A Sailor's Life," *Salem Gazette,* circa 1810 & William McCarty, *Songs, Odes, and Other Poems, on National Subjects: Part Two* (Philadelphia: Naval Compiled, WM McCarty, 1842), 74.

A Sailor Boy

5. "A Sailor Boy," *Salem Gazette,* October 29, 1805 & *The Nithsdale Minstrel: Being Original Poetry, Chiefly by the Bards of Nithsdale* (Glasgow: C. Munro & Co., 1815), 201.

A Sea Song
6. "A Sea Song," *Salem Gazette*, January 19, 1798, #674.

Heaving the Anchor
7. "Heaving the Anchor," *Salem Gazette*, August 18, 1792, #310, vol. VI.

The Fisherman's Orphan
8. "The Fisherman's Orphan," *Salem Gazette*, August 2, 1816, #62.

Written at Sea in a Heavy Gale
9. "Written at Sea in a Heavy Gale," *Salem Mercury*, February 10, 1789.

The Honest Sailor
10. "The Honest Sailor," *Salem Gazette*, October 8, 1805, #1473 & Thomas Dibdin, Collected and arranged by, *The Sailor in Songs, Naval and National of the late Charles Dibdin*, With a memoir and addenda (London: William Cloves and Sons, 1841), 236.

Harriet Low
11. Margaret C.S. Christman, "Adventurous Pursuits Americans and the China Trade 1784- 1844," (City of Washington: Smithsonian Institute Press, 1984), 96.

Again to Mary Dear
12. Bark *Sea Mew* logbook, Log 1003, Phillips Library, Peabody Essex Museum, Rowley, MA

The Seaman's Home
13. "The Seaman's Home," *Salem Gazette*, July 22, 1803, #1242 & *The Vocal Library a collection of English, Scottish and Irish Songs* (London: Printed for Sir Richard Phillips and Co. Bridge Street, Blackfriars, 1822), 572.

Come all Good People
14. Schooner *Eagle* logbook, Log 3, Phillips Library, Peabody Essex Museum, Rowley, MA

Fair Salem Town (A Seaman and His Love)

15. *Fair Salem Town (Seaman and His Love)*, Helen Hartness Flanders Ballad Collection, Special Collections, Middlebury College, Middlebury, Vermont.
16. Helen Hartness Flanders, Springfield (Vt.), Photographs 16.5 x 23.5 cm b & w photograph from the Salem Evening News circa 1922. Used with permission by Helen Hartness Flanders Ballad Collection, Special Collections, Middlebury College, Middlebury, Vermont.

Sweet William and Gentle Jenny

17. George Nichols, *Salem Ship Master and Merchant: An Autobiography, Nichols, Miss Lydia Ropes, Narrating Facts Given to Her by Her Father, George Nichols* (Salem, Mass.: The Salem Press Co., No copy write date given), 75.
18. William Abbatt, *The Magazine of History with Notes and Queries*, vol. 6 July-December 1907 (New York: 144 East 25th Street, 1907), 110 - 111.
19. Francis James Childs, *English and Scottish Popular Ballads*, Helen Child Sargent and George Lyman Kittredge, ed. (Boston and New York: Houghton Mifflin Company, Cambridge: The Riverside Press, 1904), 604.

The Disconsolate Sailor

20. *Journal of Joseph Valpey, Jr., of Salem*, November 1813 - April 1815, with other papers relating to his experience in Dartmoor prison (Detroit, Michigan: Michigan Society of Colonial Wars, Burton Historical Collection, Detroit Public Library, 1922), 44.

Living in a Seaport Town

21. Gerry Ryan, *Today and Yesteryear, Living in a Seaport Town*, Salem Sound Records, Salem, MA 2011, CD.

V. DEATH AT SEA

On The Death of a Tar

1. "On The Death of a Tar," *Salem Gazette*, July 17, 1807, #1659, #93, vol. II.
2. *Death of Frank Fid, Authentic Narrative of the Loss of His Majesty's Frigate Apollo* (London: T. Hughes Stationers, 1804), 23.

The Dying Sailor Boy

3. "The Dying Sailor Boy," *Salem Gazette*, June 11, 1811, #2067, vol. XXV & Mathew Henry Barker, *The Log Book; Or, Nautical Miscellany, By Old Sailor* (London: J&W Robins, 1930), 159.

Bury Me, Bury Me, Quick, Quick
4. Catherine, K. Piemonte, ed., *Adoniram Judson 1788-1850, Salem's Church with the Lighted Steeple, A History of the Tabernacle Church* (Salem, Massachusetts, Higginson Books Co., 2008), 137.
5. Phineas Stowe, *Ocean Melodies and Seamen's Companion, A Collection of Hymns and Music for the use of Bethels, Chaplains of the Navy and Private Devotion of Mariners* (Boston: Phineas Stowe, Publisher, No. 8 Baldwin Place, 1858), 206.

Burn the Ship
6. Alice Williams, Catherine, K. Piemonte, ed., *The Commissioning at Tabernacle Church, Salem's Church with the Lighted Steeple, A History of the Tabernacle Church* (Salem, Massachusetts, Higginson Books Co., 2008), 138.
7. "Ship News," *Essex Register*, Wednesday, February 19, 1812.
8. Phineas Stowe, *Ocean Melodies and Seamen's Companion, A Collection of Hymns and Music; for the use of Bethels, Chaplains of the Navy and Private Devotion of Mariners* (Boston: Phineas Stowe, Publisher, No. 8 Baldwin Place, 1858), 177.

Melancholy Situation... wreck of the Margaret, a friendly song
9. Jonathan Plummer, *Melancholy Situation*, Broadside collections from the Phillips Library, Rowley, MA. Printed for the author, and sold by him, 1810.

Yankee Jack
10. "Yankee Jack," *Salem Gazette*, December 30, 1808 #XXII & *Songs, Odes, and Other Poems* (Philadelphia: Complied from various sources by Wm. McCarty, 1842), 244.

Blow On! Blow On! The Pirate's Glee
11. Arthur Morrill, & Benjamin F. Baker, *Blow On! Blow On! The Pirate's Glee*, (Boston, Massachusetts, George P. Reed & Co., 1840).
12. *Blow On! Blow On! The Pirate's Glee* from Kenneth S. Goldstein Collection of American Song Broadsides Center for Popular Music, Middle Tennessee State University, retrieved online July 18, 2017, http://popmusic.mtsu.edu.

The Tale of the Sea
13. F. E. Weatherly, *The Tale of the Sea* (Salem, Massachusetts: Salem Music Co., 1885), retrieved online September 12, 2018, https://www.loc.gov/item/sm1885.12138/.

Dame Alice Was Sitting on Widow's Walk

14. *The Frank C. Brown Collection of North Carolina Folklore*, collected by Dr. Frank C. Brown during the years 1912 to 1943, in collaboration with the North Carolina Folklore Society Publisher (Durham, N.C.: Duke University Press, 1952), 139.
15. Kathy McCabe (from research prepared by Bonnie Hurd Smith, prepared for Children's Friends and Family Services.) *Boston Globe*, December 6, 2012 & Salem Links and Lore, retrieved online September 12, 2018, http://www.noblenet.org/salem/wiki/index.php/Seamen%27s_Widow_and_Orphan_Association.
16. "Church News," *Salem Evening News*, August 1, 1896.

The Mariner's Grave

17. Ship *Ringleader* logbook, Log 1906, Phillips Library, Peabody Essex Museum, Rowley, MA
18. *The Mariner's Grave*, American Old Time Song Lyrics, retrieved online November 16, 2018, http://www.traditionalmusic.co.uk/songster/16-the-mariners-grave.htm.

VI. COMMERCE

A Ship Comes in Salem

1. Oliver Jenkins, *Heavenly Bodies, A Volume of Poems by Oliver Jenkins* (Chicago: Pascal Covici, 1928), 168 & Allan Forbes & Ralph M. Eastman, *Taverns and Stagecoaches of New England vol. II* (Boston: State Street Trust Company, 1954), 62.
2. *The Granite Monthly*, a New Hampshire magazine, devoted to literature, history, and state progress (Dover, NH: Publisher H.H. Metcalf, 1928), 234.

Derby Street Salem: Present Day

3. Oliver Jenkins, *Heavenly Bodies, A Volume of Poems by Oliver Jenkins*, (Chicago: Pascal Covici, 1928), 56.

Unknown Title

4. George Granville Putman, "Salem Vessels and Their Voyages," *Essex Institute Collection vol. LIX - July 1923* (Salem, Mass.: Printed for the Essex Institute, 1923), 206.

Launching of the "Grand Turk"
5. "Launching of the Grand Turk," *Salem Gazette*, May 24, 1791 & Henry M. Brooks, *The Olden Time Series, Vol. 6: Literary Curiosities, Gleanings Chiefly from Old Newspapers of Boston and Salem, Massachusetts* (Cambridge, University Press, 1886), 119 - 120.

Th' Embargo
6. "Th' Embargo," *Salem Gazette*, February 23, 1809, #1829.

Baker's Island Light
7. Fred A. Gannon, *Old Salem Scrap Book No. 9, Stories of Salem Elders* (Salem, Mass.: Printed by Newcomb & Gauss Co. in City Hall Square for the Salem Books Co., M. F. McGrath, President), 15.

Oh Grant That Pleasant Be
8. Bark *Borneo* logbook, Log 983, Phillips Library, Peabody Essex Museum, Rowley, MA

Ye Golden Lamps of Heaven! Farewell
9. Pierre Simon Laplace, *Memoir of Nathaniel Bowditch* (Boston: Isaac R. Butts, Charles C. Little and James Brown, Publishers, 1839), 19.
10. Wikipedia contributors: Nathaniel Bowditch, Wikipedia, The Free Encyclopedia, retrieved online July 16, 2017 https://en.wikipedia.org/wiki/Nathaniel_Bowditch.
11. Sail, Power and Steam Museum, Rockland Maine, Information received on a tour by Captain Jim Sharp, chairman and founder of the museum during the summer of 2018.

VII. BOLD SEA CAPTAINS

The Fame
1. Captain Michael Rutstien, *Fame: The Salem Privateer* (Boxford, Massachusetts: Pennant Enterprises, Inc., 2006), 13.
2. John Roberts, John Rockwell, and Larry Young, *Ye Mariners All*, Goldenhindmusic, GHM-106, 2003, CD.

Bold Hathorne or "The Cruise of the Fair American"
3. *Poems of American History*, Collected by Burton Egbert Stevenson (Boston: Houghton Mifflin Company, 1908 and reprinted 1922), 670 & Rufus Griswold, *The Poets and Poetry of America* (Philadelphia: Carey and Hart), 1842.

4. Capt. Daniel "Bold Daniel" Hathorne (1730 - April 18, 1796), Burying Point Cemetery, Salem, Essex County, Massachusetts, retrieved online October 10, 2018, www.findagrave.com/memorial/8138290/daniel-hathorne.
5. Capt. Daniel "Bold Daniel" Hathorne, Salem Links and Lore, retrieved online October 10, 2018, www.noblenet.org/salem/wiki/index.php/Hathorne,_Daniel.

Manly, A Favorite New Song in the American Fleet

6. J.L. Bell, *Brave Manly's Commodore*, retrieved online June 16, 2017, http://boston1775.blogspot.com/2010/02/brave-manlys-commodore.html, Friday, February 19, 2010.
7. *Manly, A Favorite New Song in the American Fleet*, Salem Mass.: Printed and sold by E. Russell, upper end of Main-street, 1776, Phillips Library, MH 0.200, Peabody Essex Museum, Salem, MA.

Billy Taylor

8. "Impressment," *Salem Gazette*, March 30, 1813.
9. "Impressment," *Salem Gazette*, April 12, 1813.
10. *Essex Register*, Wednesday, April 7, 1813.
11. *Essex Register*, Saturday, April 10, 1813.

The Battle of Quallah Battoo

12. George Granville Putnam, *Salem Vessels and Their Voyages: A History of the Pepper Trade with the Island of Sumatra* (Salem, Massachusetts: Essex Institute Historical Collections, vol. LVII, 1922), 61.
13. *Friendship of Salem*, retrieved online June 16, 2018, www.nps.gov/sama/learn/historyculture/friendshiphistory.htm.
14. Frank A. Hitching, *Ship Registers of the District of Salem and Beverly, 1789 - 1900. Essex Institute Historical Collections, vol. XL* (Salem: Printed for the Essex Institute, Newcomb & Gauss, 1904), 195.
15. Francis Warriner, *Cruise of the United States Frigate Potomac Round the World: During the 1831 - 1834* (New York: A.M. Published by Leavitt, Lord & CO., Boston: Crocker & Brewster, 1835), 101.
16. Duane Hamilton Hurd, *History of Essex County, Massachusetts*, vol. I (Philadelphia, Pennsylvania: J. W. Lewis & Co., 1888), 79 - 80.
17. Francis Warriner, *Cruise of the United States Frigate Potomac Round the World: During the 1831 - 1834* (New York: A.M. Published by Leavitt, Lord & CO., Boston: Crocker & Brewster, 1835), 104.

Peace Party

18. "Privateering and privateering alias, the 'Peace Party' at war; alias, the Devil to pay in the Federal camp," Isaiah Thomas Broadside Ballads Project, retrieved online August 9, 2017, www.americanantiquarian.org/thomasballads/items/show/316.

The Arrival of the Remains of Lawrence and Ludlow at Salem

19. Hon. Joseph Story, *An account of the funeral honours bestowed on the remains of Capt. Lawrence and Lieut. Ludlow with the eulogy pronounced at Salem, on the occasion* (Boston: Printed by Joshua Belcher, 1813), 35.
20. *On Behalf of the Brave Capt. James Lawrence and Lieut. C. Ludlow of the Chesapeake & On the Death of Augustus C. Ludlow*, Isaiah Thomas Broadside Ballads Project, retrieved online, October 27, 2018, http://www.americanantiquarian.org/thomasballads/items/show/278.
21. "Funeral of Capt. Lawrence and Lt. Ludlow," *Essex Register*, Saturday, August 21, 1813.

The Loss off (of) Sir John Franklin

22. Ship *Ringleader* logbook, Log 1906, Phillips Library, Peabody Essex Museum, Rowley, MA
23. Robert B. Waltz and David G. Engle, *Lady Franklin's Lament (The Sailor's Dream)* (Laws K9) - Part 03, retrieved online November 20, 2018, http://www.fresnostate.edu/folklore/ballads/LK09B.html.
24. The Bodleian Library Broadside Ballad Collection, Firth c.12(81), retrieved online November 20, 2018, http://ballads.bodleian.ox.ac.uk/search/roud/487.

VIII. CAPTAIN EDWARD B. TRUMBULL

Captain Trumbull

1. Robert Booth, *History of Owners and Occupants, 90 Federal Street, Salem, Massachusetts,* Historic Salem, History of Houses in Salem, Massachusetts, retrieved online September 2017. https://hsihousehistory.omeka.net/items/show/593.
2. George Granville Putman, "Salem Vessels and Their Voyages," *Essex Institute Collection vol. LIX* (Salem, Massachusetts: Printed for the Essex Institute, Newcomb & Gauss, July 1923), 365.
3. Frank Hitchings, "Ships Registers of the Districts of Salem and Beverly," *Essex Institute Historical Collections, vol. 41* (Salem, Mass.: Printed for the Essex Institute, Newcomb & Gauss, 1905), 378.

Endnotes

4. The James Madison Carpenter Collection (AFC 1972/001), American Folklife Center, Library of Congress, Washington, D.C. & James Madison Carpenter Collection, The Vaughan Williams Memorial Library, The essential folk resource, retrieved online September 5, 2018, https://www.vwml.org/archives-catalogue/JMC. [00349 - 00351].
5. *Captain Trumbull*, The James Madison Carpenter Collection (AFC 1972/001), American Folklife Center, Library of Congress, Washington, D.C. & James Madison Carpenter Collection, The Vaughan Williams Memorial Library, The essential folk resource, retrieved online September 5, 2018, https://www.vwml.org/archives-catalogue/JMC. [00349 - 00351].
6. *Ship's Cabin Built on Roof of Hotel in Salem as Rendezvous for Famous Old Marine Society*, Boston Traveler, Friday, August 28, 1925 & Todd Balf, *Ship's Cabin, The Most Unusual Room in New England*, Yankee Magazine, November 15, 2015, retrieved online September 5, 2018, https://newengland.com/yankee-magazine/travel/massachusetts/ships-cabin-most-unusual-room/ & *Salem Links & Lore*, The Salem Marine Society, retrieved online September 5, 2018, http://www.noblenet.org/salem/wiki/index.php/Salem_Marine_Society

Tom Pepper

7. *Tom Pepper*, The James Madison Carpenter Collection (AFC 1972/001), American Folklife Center, Library of Congress, Washington, D.C. & James Madison Carpenter Collection, The Vaughan Williams Memorial Library, The essential folk resource, retrieved online September 5, 2018, https://www.vwml.org/archives-catalogue/JMC. [00349 - 00351].

Kizee Makazee - Yah or Zanzibar Work Song

8. Bark *Taria Topan* logbook, Log 1056, Phillips Library, Peabody Essex Museum, Rowley, MA
9. *Zanzibar Work Song*, The James Madison Carpenter Collection (AFC 1972/001), American Folklife Center, Library of Congress, Washington, D.C. & James Madison Carpenter Collection, The Vaughan Williams Memorial Library, The essential folk resource, retrieved online September 5, 2018, https://www.vwml.org/archives-catalogue/JMC. [03581] & [03543].

Sally Brown

10. *Sally Brown*, The James Madison Carpenter Collection (AFC 1972/001), American Folklife Center, Library of Congress, Washington, D.C. & James Madison Carpenter Collection, The Vaughan Williams Memorial Library, The essential folk resource, retrieved online September 5, 2018, https://www.vwml.org/archives-catalogue/JMC. [03236 & 03237].

Blow the Man Down

11. Lord, Breen & De Rose, *Blow the Man Down*, Popeye (Billy Costello), Melotone Records, M 13402, U.S.A., 1935.
12. *Blow the Man Down*, The James Madison Carpenter Collection (AFC 1972/001), American Folklife Center, Library of Congress, Washington, D.C. & James Madison Carpenter Collection, The Vaughan Williams Memorial Library, The essential folk resource, retrieved online September 5, 2018, https://www.vwml.org/archives-catalogue/JMC. [03236 & 03237].

Santa Anna

13. *Santa Anna*, The James Madison Carpenter Collection (AFC 1972/001), American Folklife Center, Library of Congress, Washington, D.C. & James Madison Carpenter Collection, The Vaughan Williams Memorial Library, The essential folk resource, retrieved online September 5, 2018, https://www.vwml.org/archives-catalogue/JMC. [03458].

Old Horse

14. *Old Horse*, The James Madison Carpenter Collection (AFC 1972/001), American Folklife Center, Library of Congress, Washington, D.C. & James Madison Carpenter Collection, The Vaughan Williams Memorial Library, The essential folk resource, retrieved online September 5, 2018, https://www.vwml.org/archives-catalogue/JMC. [03364].
15. Fannie Hardy Eckstorm, & Mary Winslow Smyth, *Minstrelsy of Maine: Folk Songs and Ballads of the Woods and the Coast* (Boston and New York: Houghton Mifflin Company, 1927), 223 - 225.
16. "Maine Song and Story Sampler," retrieved online October 5, 2018, https://digitalcommons.library.umaine.edu/songstorysamplercollection/27/.

One More Day

17. *One More Day*, The James Madison Carpenter Collection (AFC 1972/001), American Folklife Center, Library of Congress, Washington, D.C. & James Madison Carpenter Collection, The Vaughan Williams Memorial Library, The essential folk resource, retrieved online September 5, 2018, https://www.vwml.org/archives-catalogue/JMC. [03367].

Bound for the Rio Grande

18. *Bound for the Rio Grande*, The James Madison Carpenter Collection (AFC 1972/001), American Folklife Center, Library of Congress, Washington, D.C. & James Madison Carpenter Collection, The Vaughan Williams Memorial Library, The essential folk resource, retrieved online September 5, 2018, https://www.vwml.org/archives-catalogue/JMC. [03397].

Ruben Ranzo

19. *Ruben Ranzo,* The James Madison Carpenter Collection (AFC 1972/001), American Folklife Center, Library of Congress, Washington, D.C. & James Madison Carpenter Collection, The Vaughan Williams Memorial Library, The essential folk resource, retrieved online September 5, 2018, https://www.vwml.org/archives-catalogue/JMC. [03422].
20. *The Marine Society of Salem, Mass.* (Salem, Mass.: Newcomb & Gauss, Printers 1922), 28.

The Wide Missouri

21. *The Wide Missouri,* The James Madison Carpenter Collection (AFC 1972/001), American Folklife Center, Library of Congress, Washington, D.C. & James Madison Carpenter Collection, The Vaughan Williams Memorial Library, The essential folk resource, retrieved online September 5, 2018, https://www.vwml.org/archives-catalogue/JMC. [03467].

The Dreadnaught

22. *The Dreadnaught,* The James Madison Carpenter Collection (AFC 1972/001), American Folklife Center, Library of Congress, Washington, D.C. & James Madison Carpenter Collection, The Vaughan Williams Memorial Library, The essential folk resource, retrieved online September 5, 2018, https://www.vwml.org/archives-catalogue/JMC. [03647].
23. Stan Hugill, *Shanties From the Seven Seas* (Mystic, CT: Mystic Seaport. 2003, Original Publisher, Routledge & Kegan Paul, Inc., 1961), 346.
24. Dan Milner & Paul Kaplan, *Songs of England, Ireland, and Scotland: A Bonnie Bunch of Roses* (New York & London: Oak Publication, Sydney, 1983), 107.
25. Captain Edward B. Trumbull's Obituary, Part I, *Boston Post*, October 31, 1934.

Blow, Boys Blow

26. *Blow, Boys Blow!,* The James Madison Carpenter Collection (AFC 1972/001), American Folklife Center, Library of Congress, Washington, D.C. & James Madison Carpenter Collection, The Vaughan Williams Memorial Library, The essential folk resource, retrieved online September 5, 2018, https://www.vwml.org/archives-catalogue/JMC. [03210].
27. Captain Edward B. Trumbull's Obituary, Part II, *Boston Post*, October 31, 1934.

Hoodah Day Shanty

28. *Hoodah Day Shanty,* The James Madison Carpenter Collection (AFC 1972/001), American Folklife Center, Library of Congress, Washington, D.C. & James Madison Carpenter Collection, The Vaughan Williams Memorial Library, The essential folk resource, retrieved online September 5, 2018, https://www.vwml.org/archives-catalogue/JMC. [03371] & [03379].

Whisky Johnny

29. *Whisky Johnny*, The James Madison Carpenter collection (AFC 1972/001), American Folklife Center, Library of Congress, Washington, D.C. & James Madison Carpenter Collection, The Vaughan Williams Memorial Library, The essential folk resource, retrieved online September 5, 2018, https://www.vwml.org/archives-catalogue/JMC. [00127].
30. James Carpenter, "Lusty Chanteys From Dead Ships of Sail," *New York Times Magazine*, July 12, 1931.

My Own Country

31. *My Own Country*, The James Madison Carpenter Collection (AFC 1972/001), American Folklife Center, Library of Congress, Washington, D.C. & James Madison Carpenter Collection, The Vaughan Williams Memorial Library, The essential folk resource, retrieved online September 5, 2018, https://www.vwml.org/archives-catalogue/JMC. [00456].
32. Broadside Ballads Online. Bodleian Library Oxford, retrieved online October 10, 2018, http://ballads.bodleian.ox.ac.uk/.

Haul The Bowline

33. *Haul The Bowline*, The James Madison Carpenter Collection (AFC 1972/001), American Folklife Center, Library of Congress, Washington, D.C. & James Madison Carpenter Collection, The Vaughan Williams Memorial Library, The essential folk resource, retrieved online September 5, 2018, https://www.vwml.org/archives-catalogue/JMC. [03291].
34. John Masefield, *A Sailor's Garland* (New York: MacMillan Company), 1928, 346.
35. Captain Edward B. Trumbull's Obituary, Part III, *Boston Post*, October 31, 1934.

Bibliography

Abbatt, William. *The Magazine of History with Notes and Queries, Vol. 6.* July - December 1907. New York: 144 East 25th Street, 1907.

Adams, Bill. *I've Been Dreamin', Songs of the Sea and Sailors' Chanteys.* Edited by Robert Frothingham. Cambridge: Houghton Mifflin Co., 1924.

American Neptune: A Quarterly Journal of Maritime History and Arts. Portland, Maine: The Southworth-Anthoensen Press, Salem, Massachusetts: The American Neptune, Incorporated, 1946.

Atlas, City of Salem, Massachusetts. Philadelphia: G.M. Hopkins & Co., 1874.

Barker, Mathew Henry. *The Log Book Or, Nautical Miscellany, By Old Sailor.* London: J&W Robins, 1930.

Bertrand Harris. *The Traditional Tunes of the Child Ballads, Vol. 4 with Their Texts.* Princeton, New Jersey: Princeton University Press, 1972.

Brooks, Henry M. *The Olden Time Series, Vol. 6, Literary Curiosities, Gleanings Chiefly from Old Newspapers of Boston and Salem, Massachusetts.* Cambridge: University Press, 1886.

Brown, Frank, Collector. *The Frank C. Brown Collection of North Carolina Folklore; collected during the years 1912 to 1943, in collaboration with the North Carolina Folklore Society.* Durham, NC: Duke University Press, 1952.

Burzynski, Don. *The First Leathernecks: A Combat History of the U.S. Marines from Inception to the Halls of Montezuma.* Open Road Media, 2013.

Chappell, William. *Popular Music of the Olden Time Vol. II.* New York: Dover Publication, Inc., 1965.

Childs, Francis James. *English and Scottish Popular Ballads.* Edited from the collection of Francis James Child, by Helen Child Sargent and George Lyman Kittredge. Boston and New York: Houghton Mifflin Company, Cambridge: The Riverside Press, 1904.

Christman, Margaret C.S. *Adventurous Pursuits Americans and the China Trade 1784- 1844.* City of Washington: Smithsonian Institute Press, 1984.

Clark, Arthur H. *The Clipper Ship Era, 1843 - 1869.* New York and London: G. P. Putnam's Sons, 1911.

Clayton, Paul. *Whaling And Sailing Songs, From the Days of Moby Dick.* Tradition Records, TLP 1005, 1956, LP.

Death of Frank Fid, Authentic Narrative of the Loss of His Majesty's Frigate Apolla. London: T. Hughes stationers, 1804.

Dibdin, Thomas. Collected and arranged by, *The Sailor* in *Songs, Naval and National of the late Charles Dibdin*, With a memoir and addenda. London; William Cloves and Sons, 1841.

Doerflinger, William Main. *Songs of the Sailor and Lumberman.* Glennwood, Illinois: Meyerbooks, 3rd Edition, 1990.

Drysdale, William. *The Princess of Montserrat: Strange Narrative of Adventure and Peril on Land and Sea.* Albany, NY: Albany Book Company, 1890.

Eckstorm, Fannie Hardy and Mary Winslow Smyth. *Minstrelsy of Maine: Folk-Songs and Ballads of the Woods and the Coast.* Boston and New York: Houghton Mifflin Company, 1927.

Forbes, Allan, & Ralph M. Eastman. *Taverns and Stagecoaches of New England Vol. II.* Boston: State Street Trust Company, 1954.

Foster, Stephen. *Oh! Susanna.* New York: C., Holt, Jr., 1848.

Fowke, Edith. *The Penguin Book of Canadian Folk Songs.* Canada: Markham, Penguin Books, 1986.

Frank, Stuart M. *Jolly Sailors Bold Ballads and Songs of the American Sailor.* East Windsor, New Jersey: Camsco Music, 2010.

Frank, Stuart M. *Songs of the Sea and Shore.* Folkways Records FH 5256. New York. 1980. LP.

Frothingham, Robert, ed. *Songs of the Sea and Sailors' Chanteys.* Cambridge, MA: Houghton Mifflin Co., 1924.

Gannon, Fred A. *Old Salem Scrap Book No. 9, Stories of Salem Elders.* Salem, Mass.: Newcomb & Gauss Co. in City Hall Square, for the Salem Books Co., M. F. McGrath, President.

Gilmore, Patrick S., *On The Road To Salem.* Boston: G.P. Reed & Co., 1853.

Griswold, Rufus. *The Poets and Poetry of America.* Philadelphia: Carey and Hart. 1842.

Harlow, Frederick Pease. *Chanteying Aboard American Ships.* Barre, MA.: Barre Press, 1962.

Harlow, Frederick Pease. *The Making of a Sailor or Sea Life Aboard a Yankee Square-Rigger.* Salem: Marine Research Society of Salem, Massachusetts, 1928.

Harlow, Frederick Pease *While I'm at the Wheel, The American Neptune: A Quarterly Journal of Maritime History and Arts, Vol. VI, No. 2,* April. Portland, Maine: The Southworth-Anthoensen Press, The American Neptune, Incorporated, Salem, Massachusetts, 1946.

Haywood, Charles F. *No Ship May Sail.* Lynn, Massachusetts: Nichols-Ellis Press, 1942.

Hitching, Frank A. "Ship Registers of the District of Salem and Beverly. 1789-1900." *Essex Institute Historical Collections, Vol. XL.* Salem: Printed for the Essex Institute, Newcomb & Gauss, 1904.

Hitchings, Frank. "Ships Registers of the Districts of Salem and Beverly." *Essex Institute Historical Collections, Vol. 41*. Salem, Mass.: Printed for the Essex Institute. Newcomb & Gauss, 1905.

Howe, Elias. *Salem Quickstep. The Musician's Companion*. Boston: Oliver Diston & Co., Washington Street Publication, 1842.

Hugill, Stan. *Shanties From the Seven Seas*. Mystic, CT: Mystic Seaport, 2003, Original Publisher, Routledge & Kegan Paul, Inc., 1961.

Hull, Asa. *Gleanings of Sacred Song: Suitable for Gospel Meetings, Praise Meetings, Sunday Schools and Young People's Societies*. New York: Asa Hull, 1892.

Huntington, Gale. *Songs the Whalemen Sang*. New York: Barre Publishing Company, Dover Publications, Inc., 1970. First Printed 1964.

Hurd, Duane Hamilton. *History of Essex County, Massachusetts Vol. I*. Philadelphia, Pennsylvania: J. W. Lewis & Co., 1888.

Jenkins, Oliver. *Heavenly Bodies, A Volume of Poems by Oliver Jenkins*. Chicago: Pascal Covici, 1928.

John Jewett's, *National Flutina and Accordion Teacher: Complete Book of Instructions*. Boston: Oliver Diston & Co., Washington Street Publication, 1850.

Journal of a Voyage Barque San Francisco 1849 - 1850. Captain Thomas Remmonds, On display at the Beverly Historical Society, Beverly, Massachusetts.

Journal of Joseph Valpey, Jr., of Salem. November, 1813 -April, 1815, with other papers relating to his experience in Dartmoor prison, Michigan Society of Colonial Wars, Burton Historical Collection, Detroit Public Library, 1922.

Kaplan, Larry. *Furthermore*. Hannah Lane Music, 2016. CD.

Laplace, Pierre Simon. *Memoir of Nathaniel Bowditch*. Isaac R. Butts, Charles C. Little and James Brown, Publishers, 1839.

Lord, Breen, De Rose. *Blow the Man Down*. Popeye (Billy Costello), Melotone Records, M 13402, U.S.A., 1935.

Marine Society of Salem, Mass. Salem, Mass.: Newcomb & Gauss, Printers 1922.

Masefield, John. *A Sailor's Garland*. New York: MacMillan Company, 1928.

Manly, A Favorite New Song in the American Fleet. Salem Mass.: Printed and sold by E. Russell, upper end of Main-street, 1776, Phillips Library, Peabody Essex Museum, Salem, MA.

Mason, Lowell. *Carmina Sacra: or, Boston Collection of Church Music: comprising the most popular psalm and hymn tunes in eternal use together with a great variety of new tunes, chants, sentences, motetts*. Boston: J. H. Wilkins & R. B. Carter, 1841.

McCarty, William. *Songs, Odes, and Other Poems, on National Subjects: Part Two*. Philadelphia: Naval Compiled, WM McCarty, 1842.

Milner, Dan and Paul Kaplan. *Songs of England, Ireland, and Scotland: A Bonnie Bunch of Roses.* New York, London and Sydney: Oak Publication, 1983.

Nichols, George. *Salem Ship Master and Merchant: An Autobiography, Nichols, Miss Lydia Ropes, Narrating Facts Given to Her by Her Father, George Nichols.* Salem, Mass.: The Salem Press Co., No copyright date given.
Nithsdale Minstrel: Being Original Poetry, Chiefly by the Bards of Nithsdale, C. Glasgow: Munro & Co., 1815.

Paine, Ralph D. *The Ships and Sailors of Old Salem.* New York: The Outing Publishing Company, 1908.
Peabody, Alfred. *On The Early Days and Rapid Growth of California.* Salem, Massachusetts: Essex Institute Historical Collection Vol. 12-13 Essex Institute, The Salem Press, 1872.
Piemonte, Catherine, K. *Adoniram Judson 1788 - 1850, Salem's Church with the Lighted Steeple, A History of the Tabernacle Church.* Salem, Massachusetts: Higginson Books Co., 2008.
Pierpont, James, and John P. Ordway. *The Returned Californian.* Boston: E. H. Wade, monographic, 1852.
Pike, Marshall S. *Home Again.* Salem, MA: J. Peckham, 1858.
Plummer, Jonathan. *Melancholy Situation.* Broadside collections, Phillips Library, Rowley, MA. Printed for the author, and sold by him, 1810.
Poems of American History. Collected by Stevenson, Burton Egbert, Boston: Houghton Mifflin Company, 1908 and reprinted 1922.
Poetical Works of Sir Walter Scott: With a Sketch of His Life By Sir Walter Scott. Philadelphia: J. W. Lake and J Crissy, No. 4 Minor Street and Thomas Cowperthwait & Co No. 263 Market Street, 1838.
Putman, George Granville. "Salem Vessels and Their Voyages." *Essex Institute Collection Vol. LIX - July.* Salem, Mass.: Printed for the Essex Institute, 1923.
Putnam, George Granville. "Salem Vessels and Their Voyages: A History of the Pepper Trade with the Island of Sumatra." *Essex Institute Historical Collections, Vol. LVII.* Salem, Mass:, 1922.
Putman, George Granville. "Salem Vessels and Their Voyages." *Essex Institute Collection Vol. LIX - July.* Salem, Mass:, Essex Institute, Newcomb & Gauss, 1923.

Rantoul, Robert. *Old-Time Ships of Salem.* Boston: C.B. Webster & Co. Salem, Massachusetts: Essex Institute, 1917.
Roberts, John, Rockwell, John, and Young, Larry. *Ye Mariners All.* Goldenhindmusic. GHM-106. 2003. CD.

Robotti, Francis Diane. *Whaling and Old Salem*. New York: Fountainhead Publishers, 1962.

Rutstien, Captain Michael. *Fame The Salem Privateer*. Boxford, Massachusetts: Pennant Enterprises, Inc., 2006.

Ryan, Gerry. *Today and Yesteryear*. Salem Sound Records. Salem, MA 2011. CD.

Ryan, William Bradbury. *Ryan's Mammoth Collection: 1050 Reels and Jigs*. Boston: Elias Howe, 1883.

Sailor's Magazine and Naval Journal, Vol. 5. American Seamen's Friend Society, Published by American Seamen's Friend Society, 1833.

Sanders, Charles Walton. *Union Fifth Reader: Embracing a Full Exposition of the Principles of Rhetorical Reading*. New York and Chicago: Ivison, Blakeman, Taylor & Co., Publishers, 1876.

Shay, Frank. *American Sailor's Treasury: Sea Chanteys, Legends and Lore*. New York: Smithmark Publishers, Inc., 1991.

Silsbee Family Papers, MSS 74, Phillips Library, Peabody Essex Museum, Salem, Mass.

Silsbee, Nathaniel. *Biographical Notes*, Salem Collection, Salem Public Library, title page missing, no publication information available.

Silber, Irwin. *Songs of the Great American West*. New York: The Macmillan Company, 1967.

Sky, Patrick, ed., *Ryan's Mammoth Collection of Fiddle Tunes, 1050 Reels and Jigs*. Pacific, MO: Mel Bay, 1965, Originally Published Boston, Massachusetts: Publisher Elias Howe, 1883.

Songs, Odes, and Other Poems. Complied from various sources by Wm. McCarty. Philadelphia: 1842.

Starboard List. *Songs of the Tall Ships & Cruising 'Round Yarmouth*. Genes Records. GCD 1025/27. 1996. CD.

Story, Hon. Joseph. *An account of the funeral honours bestowed on the remains of Capt. Lawrence and Lieut. Ludlow with the eulogy pronounced at Salem, on the occasion*. Boston: Printed by Joshua Belcher, 1813.

Stowe, Phineas. *Ocean Melodies and Seamen's Companion, A Collection of Hymns and Music; for the use of Bethels, Chaplains of the Navy and Private Devotion of Mariners*. Boston: Published by Phineas Stowe, No. 8 Baldwin Place, 1858.

Sweet, Ralph, ed. *The Fifer's Delight*. Enfield CT: 1981 Originally Published. 1966.

Vocal Library a Collection of English, Scottish and Irish Songs. London: Printed for Sir Richard Phillips and Co. Bridge Street, Blackfriars, 1822.

Ward, Anna Lydia. *Surf and Wave: The Sea as Sung by the Poets.* New York: T.Y. Crowell & Co., 1883.

Warriner, Francis. *Cruise of the United States Frigate Potomac Round the World: During the 1831 - 1834.* New York: A.M. Published by Leavitt, Lord & CO., Boston: Crocker & Brewster, 1835.

White, Eugene, Richard. *Songs for Good Fighting.* London: Elkin Mathews, Vigo Street, 1908.

Web Resources

American Antiquarian Society
www.americanantiquarian.org
Around the Horn
www.larcomfamilytree.com
Broadside Ballads Bodleian Libraries Oxford University
www.ballads.bodleian.ox.ac.uk
California State Library
www.library.ca.gov
Cecil Sharp House
www.vwml.org
Center for Popular Music Middle Tennessee State University
www.popmusic.mtsu.edu
City of Salem
www.salem.com
Collections Research Center at Mystic Seaport
www.research.mysticseaport.org
Dalton, Jim & Smith-Dalton, Maggi
www.singingstring.org
David M. Rubenstein Rare Book & Manuscript Library at Duke University
www.library.duke.edu
Find A Grave
www.findagrave.com.
Friendship of Salem
www.nps.gov
Google Books
www.books.google.com

Harris Broadside Collection, Brown University Library
www.repository.library.brown.edu
Hathi Trust Digital Library
www.catalog.hathitrust.org
Helen Hart Flanders Collection, Middlebury College
www.middlebury.edu
Historic Beverly
www.historicbeverly.net
History of Owners and Occupants, Historic Salem History of Houses in Salem, Massachusetts
www.historicsalem.org
Internet Archive
www.archive.org
Isaiah Thomas Broadside Ballads
www.americanantiquarian.org
James Madison Carpenter Collection
www.loc.gov and www.vwml.org
Journal of American Folklore
www.jstor.org
Lester S. Levy Collection of Sheet Music, Johns Hopkins University
www.levysheetmusic.mse.jhu.edu
Library of Congress
www.loc.gov
Maine Song and Story Sampler
www.digitalcommons.library.umaine.edu

Mainly Folk: English Folk and Other Good Music
www.mainlynorfolk
Marine Society at Salem
www.marinesocietysalem.org
Mary Barker, Photographer
www.mabarkerphotography.com
Mudcat
www.mudcat.org
Mystic Seaport Museum
www.research.mysticseaport.org
Phillip's Library Rowley/ Salem, Massachusetts
www.pem.org
Poetry & Song on the Outbreak of War
www.americainclass.org
Popular Songs of the Day
www.loc.gov
Providence Public Library
www.provlib.org
Registry of Deeds
www.salemdeeds.com
Rosie Strom - Graphic Designer
www.rosiestromdesign.com
Sail Power Steam Museum, Rockland Maine
www.sailpowersteammuseum.org
Salem Links and Lore, Salem Public Library
www.noblenet.org/salem/wiki/index.php/Main_Page
Salem, Massachusetts
www.salemweb.com
Streets of Salem
www.streetsofsalem.com

Traditional Ballad Index, Fresno State University
www.fresnostate.edu
Traditional Music Library
www.traditionalmusic.co.uk
The Traditional Tune Archive
www.tunearch.org
Trial Pamphlets Collection, Cornell University Law Library
www.awcollections.library.cornell.edu
USGenNet
www.usgennet.org
Word on the Street
www.digital.nls.uk
Vaughan Williams Memorial Library
www.vwml.org

Blog

J.L. Bell, Brave Manly's Commodore, http://boston1775.blogspot.com/2010/02/brave-manlys-commodor.html.

Shipping and Prison Log Journals

Journal of Joseph Valpey, Jr., of Salem, November, 1813 - April, 1815, with other papers relating to his experience in Dartmoor prison. Detroit, Michigan: Michigan Society of Colonial Wars, Burton Historical Collection, Detroit Public Library, 1922.

Schooner *Eagle* logbook, Log 3, Phillips Library, Peabody Essex Museum, Rowley, MA

Ship *Astrea* logbook, Log 11, Phillips Library, Peabody Essex Museum, Rowley, MA

Ship *George* logbook, Log 291, Phillips Library, Peabody Essex Museum, Rowley, MA

Ship *Bengal* logbook, Log 302, Phillips Library, Peabody Essex Museum, Rowley, MA

Ship *Bengal*, # 65 Nicholson Whaling Collection, Providence Public Library, Providence, RI

Bark *La Grange* logbook, Log 621, Passenger Journal, Phillips Library, Peabody Essex Museum, Rowley, MA

Ship *America* logbook, Log 918, Phillips Library, Peabody Essex Museum, Rowley, MA

Bark *Borneo* logbook, Log 983, Phillips Library, Peabody Essex Museum, Rowley, MA

Bark *La Grange* logbook, Log 1001, Phillips Library, Peabody Essex Museum, Rowley, MA

Bark *Sea Mew* logbook, Log 1003, Phillips Library, Peabody Essex Museum, Rowley, MA

Bark *Taria Topan* logbook, Log 1056, Phillips Library, Peabody Essex Museum, Rowley, MA

Ship *Vaughan* logbook, Log 1057, Phillips Library, Peabody Essex Museum, Rowley, MA

Bark *La Grange* logbook, Log 1702, Phillips Library, Peabody Essex Museum, Rowley, MA

Ship *Ringleader* logbook, Log 1906, Phillips Library, Peabody Essex Museum, Rowley, MA

Chapter Tune References

Chapter 1: *Oh! Susanna* by Stephen Foster. *Oh Susanna* (New York: C., Holt, Jr., 1848). Library of Congress, Stephen Foster, retrieved online December 20, 2018 https://www.loc.gov/item/ihas.200035701.

Chapter 2: *On The Road To Salem* by Patrick Gilmore. *On The Road To Salem*. Patrick Gilmore. (Boston: G.P. Reed & Co., 1853). Courtesy of the Boston Public Library.

Chapter 3: *Salem Quickstep*. Elias Howe. *The Musician's Companion* (Boston: Oliver Diston & Co., Washington Street Publication, 1842), 79 & John Jewett's, *National Flutina and Accordion Teacher: Complete Book of Instructions* (Boston: Oliver Diston & Co., Washington Street Publication, 1850), 36. Courtesy of the Boston Public Library.

Chapter 4: *Salem Hornpipe* by Patrick S. Gilmore. Patrick Sky, ed., *Ryan's Mammoth Collection Fiddle Tunes* (Pacific, MO: MelBay Publication, 1995, originally published in Boston, 1883), 120 & Jim Dalton's personal collection.

Chapter 5: *The Salem Artillery*. Transcribed by T. William Smith, Essex Institute, circa 1980.

Chapter 6: *Harriet Low* by Daisy Nell. Transcribed by T. William Smith. Daisy Nell's personal collection.

Chapter 7: *Ye Golden Lamps of Heaven! Farewell* by Philip Doddridge, tune by Henry K. Oliver. *Gleanings of Sacred Song: Suitable for Gospel Meetings, Praise Meetings, Sunday Schools and Young People's Societies* (New York: Asa Hull, 1892), 193. Courtesy of the Boston Public Library.

Chapter 8. *Federal Street* by Henry K. Oliver. *Carmina Sacra: or, Boston Collection of Church Music: comprising the most popular psalm and hymn tunes in eternal use together with a great variety of new tunes, chants, sentences, motetts*. Boston: J. H. Wilkins & R. B. Carter, 1841, 84. Courtesy of the Boston Public Library.

Photographs, Postcards, Clippings, Maps

Cover: The *Friendship*, MARY BARKER - Photographer * 1: *Oh! Susanna*, Stephen Foster tune for *I Come From Salem City*, BOSTON PUBLIC LIBRARY * 2: Derby Wharf, Salem Map, 1874, BETSEY & ED BENNETT'S Personal Collection * 5: *The California Gold Diggers*, Jesse Hutchinson, LESTER S. LEVY COLLECTION OF SHEET MUSIC * 9: On the Banks of the Sacramento, Carpenter Collection, LIBRARY OF CONGRESS * 12: To the Traveling Public, *SALEM GAZETTE* & CHRISTINE ELIZABETH MISTRETTA'S Personal Collection * 15: John Bertram House, MARY BARKER - Photographer * 16: *Witch of the Wave*, RYAN'S MAMOUTH COLLECTION * 17: La Grange as a Prison ship in San Francisco Harbor, CALIFORNIA STATE LIBRARY * 20: *The Returned Californian*, James Pierpont, LIBRARY OF CONGRESS * 22: *On The Road To Salem*, Patrick S. Gilmore, BOSTON PUBLIC LIBRARY * 24: Mermaid Salem, Benjamin Franklin West Painting, MUSEUM OF FINE ARTS * 30: The *Friendship*, MARY BARKER - Photographer * 32: *Salem Quick Step*, Elias Howe, *The Musician's Companion*, BOSTON PUBLIC LIBRARY * 44: Whale Oil on Union Wharf and 25 Young Men Wanted, SALEM GAZETTE * 45: Ship *Bengal*, # 65 Nicholson Whaling Collection, PROVIDENCE PUBLIC LIBRARY * 46: Broadside of the Salem Bicentennial, AUTHOR'S Personal Collection * 54: Nathaniel Silsbee, SALEM PUBLIC LIBRARY HISTORICAL ROOM * 56: *Salem Hornpipe*, P.S. Gilmore, RYAN'S MAMMOTH COLLECTION, JIM and MAGGI DALTON'S Private Collection * 59: *Home Again*, KENNETH S. GOLDSTEIN COLLECTION OF AMERICAN SONG BROADSIDES * 60: *The Seaman*, SALEM GAZETTE * 61: *The Sailor's Watch At Sea*, SALEM GAZETTE * 65: *A Sea Song*, SALEM GAZETTE * 66: The Anchor at Cabot Farm, Salem, Massachusetts, AUTHOR'S Personal Collection * 69: *The Fisherman's Orphan*, SALEM GAZETTE * 73: *The Honest Sailor*, SALEM GAZETTE * 77: *The Seaman's Home*, SALEM GAZETTE * 79: Derby Wharf, AUTHOR'S Personal Collection * 80: Portrait of a young Helen Hartness Flanders, *Salem Evening News*, HELEN HARTNESS BALLAD COLLECTION, MIDDLEBURY COLLEGE

* 80: Transcription of *Fair Salem Town*, HELEN HARTNESS BALLAD COLLECTION, MIDDLEBURY COLLEGE * 87: Ropes, Peabody and Putman Wharf, Salem Map, 1874, BETSEY & ED BENNETT'S Personal Collection * 88: *Salem Artillery*, T. WILLIAM SMITH'S Personal Collection * 90: *On The Death of a Tar*, SALEM GAZETTE * 92: Winter Island Lighthouse, MARY BARKER - Photographer * 94: *The Caravan*, TABERNACLE CHURCH'S HISTORIC ROOM * 96: Tabernacle Church, TABERNACLE CHURCH'S HISTORIC ROOM * 97: The Missionary Bench, TABERNACLE CHURCH'S HISTORIC ROOM * 100: *The Margaret*, OLD-TIME SHIPS OF SALEM * 102: *Yankee Jack*, SALEM GAZETTE * 104: *The Tale of the Sea* by F. E. Weatherly LIBRARY OF CONGRESS * 107: Salem Map, 1820, AUTHOR'S Personal Collection * 108: Widow's Walk at 174 Derby Street, Hawkes House, MARY BARKER - Photographer * 109: Outward Bound, AUTHOR'S Personal Collection * 109: Cleopatra, AUTHOR'S Personal Collection * 109: Ship St. Paul, AUTHOR'S Personal Collection * 111: The Mariner's Grave by Glenn Church, AUTHOR'S Personal Collection * 112: *Harriet Low*, by Daisy Nell, transcribed by T. William Smith * 114: Derby Street, Salem Map, 1874, BETSEY & ED BENNETT'S Personal Collection * 116: Derby Wharf, MARY BARKER - Photographer * 119: The Grand Turk, AUTHOR'S Personal Collection * 120: Custom House, MARY BARKER - Photographer * 121: Central Wharf, Salem Map, 1874, BETSEY & ED BENNETT'S Personal Collection * 123: Baker's Island, SAL PANGALLO'S Personal Collection * 124: Bowditch House, MARY BARKER - Photographer * 126: *Ye Golden Lamps* by Philip Doddridge music by H.K. Oliver GLEANINGS OF SACRED SONG: *Suitable for Gospel Meetings, Praise Meetings, Sunday Schools*, BOSTON PUBLIC LIBRARY * 129: The Fame, MARY BARKER - Photographer * 132: Hathorne's Grave at the Charter Street Burying Point, MARY BARKER - Photographer * 136: *Impressment*, part I, SALEM GAZETTE * 136: *Impressment*, part II, SALEM GAZETTE * 140: Figurehead on The Friendship, MARY BARKER - Photographer * 145: The *Friendship* and the *Adventure* in dry-dock, MARY BARKER - Photographer * 146: *Capture of the Brig Dispatch*, part I, SALEM GAZETTE * 149: *Capture of the Brig Dispatch*,

part II, *SALEM GAZETTE* * 151: *Funeral of Capt. Lawrence and Lt. Ludlow*, ESSEX REGISTER * 154: *Federal Street*, by Henry K. Oliver, Lowell Mason's *Carmina*, BOSTON PUBLIC LIBRARY * 156: Captain Edward B. Trumbull, SALEM MARINE SOCIETY * 157: *Captain Trumbull*, LIBRARY OF CONGRESS & VAUGHAN WILLIAMS MEMORIAL LIBRARY AT THE CECIL SHARP HOUSE - THE JAMES MADISON CARPENTER COLLECTION * 158: *Ship's Cabin Built on Roof of Hotel in Salem as Rendezvous for Famous Old Marine Society*, BOSTON TRAVELER * 159: Hawthorne Hotel Salem Marine Room, AUTHOR'S Personal Collection * 159: Hawthorne Hotel, AUTHOR'S Personal Collection * 159: Architect's drawing of the Salem Marine Society's, Hall, SALEM MARINE SOCIETY * 160: *Tom Pepper*, LIBRARY OF CONGRESS & VAUGHANWILLIAMS MEMORIAL LIBRARY AT THE CECIL SHARP HOUSE - THE JAMES MADISON CARPENTER COLLECTION * 166: *Blow the Man Down*, LIBRARY OF CONGRESS & VAUGHAN WILLIAMS MEMORIAL LIBRARY AT THE CECIL SHARP HOUSE - THE JAMES MADISON CARPENTER COLLECTION * 171: *Taria Topan*, SAL PANGALLO'S Personal Collection * 172: Captain Edward B. Trumbull's Home at 90 Federal Street, MARY BARKER - Photographer * 175: *The Wide Missouri*, LIBRARY OF CONGRESS & VAUGHAN WILLIAMS MEMORIAL LIBRARY AT THE CECIL SHARP HOUSE - THE JAMES MADISON CARPENTER COLLECTION * 177: Captain Edward B. Trumbull's obituary transcribed, *BOSTON POST* * 179: Captain Edward B. Trumbull's obituary transcribed, *BOSTON POST* * 180: *Hoodah Day Shanty*, LIBRARY OF CONGRESS & VAUGHAN WILLIAMS MEMORIAL LIBRARY AT THE CECIL SHARP HOUSE - THE JAMES MADISON CARPENTER COLLECTION * 182: *Whisky Johnny*, LIBRARY OF CONGRESS & VAUGHAN WILLIAMS MEMORIAL LIBRARY AT THE CECIL SHARP HOUSE - THE JAMES MADISON CARPENTER COLLECTION * 187: Captain Edward B. Trumbull's obituary transcribed, *BOSTON POST* * 189: Pete Seeger on Derby Wharf, with Daisy Nell, Bill and Sarah Smith, JIM McALLISTER'S Private Collection

Index

- A -

A Sailor Boy, 63-64
A Sailor's Garland, 186
A Sailor's Life, 62-63
A Sea Song, 65
A Ship Comes In
 Salem 1830, 114
A Song, 102
A Song Concerning Love, 50
Active, Ship, 82
Adams, Bill, 10-11
Adoniram Judson,
 Salem's Church with the
 Lighted Steeple, A History of
 the Tabernacle Church, 94-97
Adventure, The, 145
Adventurous Pursuits Americans
 and the China Trade 1784-
 1844, , 74, 75
Again to Mary Dear, 75-76
Akbar, xx
Alexander, Daniel Asher, 39
America, Ship, 35-36
American Neptune, xxii
American Old Tyme
 Song Lyrics, 110-111
American Sailor's Treasury: Sea
 Chanteys, Legends and Lore, 2
An account of the funeral
 honours bestowed on the
 remains of Capt. Lawrence
 and Lieut. Ludlow with the
 eulogy pronounced at Salem,
 on the occasion, 150-151

Andover Seminary, 94
Ann, Brig, 117
Apollo, 90
Aristide, Ship, 94
Astrea, Ship, 53, 54

- B -

Baker's Island, 122
Baker's Island Light, 122
Balf, Todd, 214
Banks of the Sacramento, xvii, 180
Barker, Nathan, 6
Battle of Quallah Battoo, The,
 140-145
Battle of the Peace Party, 146
Beachman, Edward, 78
Bell Bottom Trousers, 184
Bell, J.L., 133
Bengal, Ship, xix, 44-45, 46, 50
Bertram, John, 2, 12-15
Beverly Historical Society, 4
Billy Taylor, 136-139
Blow, Boys, Blow!, 178-179
Blow! Oh Blow!, 52
Blow on! Blow on!
 The Pirate's Glee, 103-104
Blow The Man Down, 166-167
Bodleian Library Broadside
 Ballad Collection, 152
Bold Daniel, 130
Bold Hathorne, 130-132
Bold Richard, 128
Bonny Parte, xx
Booth, Robert, 156
Borneo, Bark, 52, 123
Boston Post, 177, 179, 187

Boston Traveler, 159
Bound For the Rio Grande,
 170-171
Bounding Billows, 98
Bowditch, Nathaniel, 124
Briggs, Enos, 118, 140
Brookhouse, Robert, 75
Brooks, Rev. Charles Timothy,
 117
Brooks, Henry M., 117
Burn the Ships, 97-99
Bury Me, Bury Me,
 Quick, Quick, 94-95
Bury Me, Bury Me,
 Quick, Quick Part II, 96

- C -

Cahoon, Stephen, 50
California Gold Diggers, The,
 5-9, 180
California Song, The, 2
Californian, The, 6, 8, 180
Camptown Races, xvii, 9, 180
Captain's Glen's Unhappy
 Voyage To New Barbary, 90
Captain Calls All
 Hands, The, 50-51
Captain Trumbull, 156-187
Carlton, Rev. Michael, 106
Carmina Sacra, 7
Carpenter, James Madison, 9,
 156-187
Caravan, Ship, 94, 97, 98
Castigator, 146

Chanteying Aboard American
 Ships, xx
Chappell, William, 24 Charter
 Street Burying Point, 132
Cheever, James, 35
Chesapeake, 150-151
Child Ballads, 24, 82, 106
Child, Francis James, 24, 82, 106
Children's Friends Society, 106
Chinnery, George, 74, 75
Christman, Margaret C.S., 74, 75
Clark, Arthur H., 12-15
Clark, Stephen G., 146
Clayton, Paul, 24
Cleopatra, 109
Clipper Ship Era.
 1843 - 1869, 12-15
Come All Good People, 78-79
Come Down You Blood
 Red Roses, xxiii
Connecticut Mirror, 136
Costello, Billy, 163
Crowinshield, G., 35, 151
Cruel Ship's Carpenter, 29
Cruise of the Fair
 American, The, 30
Cruising 'Round Yarmouth, 46
Custom House, 120

- D -

Daemon Lover, 29
Dame Alice Was Sitting on
 Widow's Walk, 106-108
Dan Emmett, 5

Index

Dartmore Prison, 39-40, 41, 2, 84
David M. Rubenstein Rare Book & Manuscript Library at Duke University, 58
De Boatman Dance, 6
Death of Frank Fid, Authentic Narrative of the Loss of His Majesty's Frigate Apollo, 90
Derby, Elias Hasket, 53, 54
Derby Street - Salem: Present Day, 115-116
Derby Wharf, 117
Dibdin, Charles, 72
Disconsolate Sailor, The, 84-85
Dispatch, Brig, 146
Dixie Isle, xxi
Dodge, Ernest, xx
Dodge, Pickering, 44
Doddridge, Philip, 124
Doerflinger, William Main, xxii, xxvi, 9
Doten, Mrs. Ella, 80
Downers, Captain John, 145
Dreadnaught, The, 176-177
Dying Sailor Boy, The, 92-93

- E -

Eagle, Schooner, 78
Eckstorm, Fannie Hardy, 168
Eliza, 2
Endicott, Captain Charles, 145
Endicott, Governor John, 117
English and Scottish Popular Ballads, 24, 82, 106
Erebus, 152

Essex Fire and Marine Ins., 124
Essex Register, 98, 118, 139, 151

- F -

Fair American, 130
Fair Salem Town (Seaman and His Love), 80-81
Fairchild, Captain, 100
Faithful Sailor, The, 54-55
Fame of Salem, The, 128-129
Fame; The Salem Privateer, 128-129
Fisherman's Orphan, The, 68-69
Flanders, Helen Hartness, 80
Forecastle Songs and Chanties, xxv, 9, 156
Foster, Stephen, xxii, 3, 9, 180
Frank C. Brown Collection of North Carolina Folklore, 106
Frank, Stuart M., 50
Franklin, Captain Sir John, 152
Friendship, The, 140, 141, 145
Frigate Potomac, 141
Frothingham, Robert, 10-11
Fruits of Gambling's, The, 42-43
Funeral of Capt. Lawrence and Lt. Ludlow, 150-151

- G -

Gam, More Songs the Whalemen Sang, xix
Gannon, Fred A., 122
Gentle Annie, xvii
George Nichols: Salem Ship Master and Merchant, 82

George, Ship, 50
Gilmore, Patrick, 20
Girl Who'd Choose a Sailor, The
   72-73
Gloucester, MA, 50
Glover, John, 39
Gold, 17
Gold Hunters Story, The, 18, 19
Gosport Tragedy, The, 29-31
Grand Turk, Brig, 118-119
Greenland Whale, The, 46-48
Greenland Whale
   Fisheries, The, 46-48
Gwine to Run All Night, 180

- H -

Hadley Rescue Mission, 107
Halifax, Nova Scotia, 150-151
Hall Gordon, 97
Harlow, Frederick Pease,
   xx-xxiii, 9
Harmony Grove Cemetery, 14
Harriet Low, 74, 75
Harris, Bertrand, 24
Harvard University, 156
Hathorne, Captain Daniel, 130
Haul Away Joe, 157
Haul The Bowline, 186
Hawthorne Hotel, 158-159
Hawthorne, Nathaniel, 130
Heard, Ship, 151
Hearts of Gold, xix
Heaving the Anchor, 66-67
Heavenly Bodies, A Volume of
   Poems by Oliver Jenkins, 98
Henry VIII, 186

Henry, Brig, 151
Henry, Sam, xix
Hills of Georgetown, 34-35
Ho! Boys! Ho!, 5, 7-9, 181
Home Again, 58-59
Home Boys Home, 184
Honest Sailor, The, 72-73
Hoodah Day Shanty, 9, 180-181
Hugill, Stan, xxii
Humphreys, Edwin, 110, 152
Hunt, Chat, 18-19
Hunt, William, 75
Hunting for Lice and Fleas, 41
Huntington, Gale, 46, 49, 50
Hutchison, Jr., Jesse, 5-9

- I -

I Came From Salem City, xvii, 2-4
Impressment, 136-139
Isaiah Thomas Broadside
   Ballads Project, 54, 146
I've Been Dreamin', 10-11

- J -

Jabbour, Alan, 16
Jackson, President Andrew, 145
James Madison Carpenter
   Collection, 156-187
Jenkins, Oliver, 114, 115-116
Jingle Bells, 20
Jones, David, 46
Journal of Joseph Valpey, Jr., 39,
   41, 42, 84
Judson, Adoniram, 94, 97, 98

Index

- K -

Kaplan, Larry, xix, 49
Kitfield, A.E., 61
Kittredge, George Lyman, 156
Kizee Makazee-Yah, 164-165

- L -

Lady Alice, 106
Lady Franklin's Lament, 152
Lady Franklin's Lament For Her Husband, 152
La Grange, Bark, 5, 6, 17, 18-19, 34-35, 37
Leary, Thomas, 106
Launching of the Grand Turk, 118-119
Lawrence, Captain, 150-151
Lee, Schooner, 133
Lester Levy Sheet Music Collection, 5, 103
Lieutenant Ludlow, 150-151
Liddell, Richard D., 104
Lines composed on a Court Martial of Oliver Poland, 35
Liverpool, England, 177, 180
Living in a Seaport Town, 86-87
Log Book; Or, Nautical Miscellany, By Old Sailor, 92
Lordholm, Captain, 12
Loss of His Majesty's Frigate Apollo, 90
Loss off (of) Sir John Franklin, The, 152, 153
Lotus, 49
Low, Harriet, 74, 75

- M -

Madison, President James, 146
Magazine of History with Notes and Queries, 82
Magee, James, 53
Making of a Sailor, The, xx, xxiii, 9
Manley, Captain John, 133
Manly, A Favorite New Song in the American Fleet, 133-135
Margaret, Ship, 100
Marine Society at Salem, xxv, 158, 158-159, 172, 187
Marine Society Bethel, 107
Mariner's Grave, The, 110-111
Marston, Peter, 46
Mary My Dear, 76
Masefield, John, 186
McCarty, William, 62
McClusky, John, 106
Melancholy Situation, 100-101
Mermaid, The, 24-26
Merrily, Merrily!, 52
Middlebury College Special Collections and Archives, 80
Miller, Edward F., 156
Millet, Captain Charles, 117
Minstrelsy of Maine, 168
Monkey, Schooner, 39
Monroe, President James, 145, 151
Morgan, William F., 7, 17, 18-19, 34-35
Morning Light, 152
Morrill, Arthur, 103
My Own Country, 184-185

Mt. Auburn Cemetery, 124
Mugford, Charles, D., 51

- N -

National Park Service, 140
Nell, Daisy, 74, 75
New American Practical
   Navigator, The, 124
New York Times, 182
Newburyport, MA, 176
Newel, Samuel, 97
Nichols, George, 82, 141
Nichols, Ichabod, 141
Nicholas, Jonathan, 13
Nichols, Miss Lydia Ropes, 82
Nighsdale Minstrel, 63
Nott, Samuel, 97

- O -

O You Whose Lives, 77
O'Hegarty, Charles, 46
Occasioned by the arrival of the
   remains of Lawrence and
   Ludlow at Salem, 150-151
Ocean Melodies and Seamen's
   Companion, 196
Of the Lost Ship, 27-28
Of Dartmore Prison, 39-40
Oh California, 2
Oh Dear, What Can
   The Matter Be?, 120
Oh Grant That Pleasant Be, 123
Oh' Susanna, xvii, 2, 4
Old Folks at Home, xvii
Old Horse, 166-167

Old Salem Scrap Book No. 9, 122
Olden Time Series, Vol. 6
On The Death of A Tar, 90-91
On the Loss of the Schooner
   Machanic Captain
   Holland, 49
One More Day, 169
Ordway, John P., 20-21, 58
Outward Bound, Ship, 109
Outward Bound, Songs From
   the James Madison Carpenter
   Collection, 160

- P -

Paine, Ralph Delahaye, 191
Peabody, Alfred, 2, 12
Peabody, Joseph, 44, 51
Peace Party, 146-149
Peckman, J., 58
Peirpont, James, 20-21
Penguin Book of Canadian
   Folk Songs, The, 29-31
Phelps, Rev. S. D., 37
Pickman, Benjamin, 44
Piemonte, Catherine, K., 94, 97
Pierce Benjamin, 141
Pierce, Henry, 141
Pike, Marshall S., 58
Plummer, Jonathan, 100-101
Poems of American History,
   199, 208
Polly, Ship, 50
Popeye, 166
Popular Music of the
   Olden Time, 24
Portland, Maine, 141, 168

Index

Potomac, USS, 145
Pretty Polly, 29
Prince, Henry, 117
Princess of Montserrat, 53

- R -

Red Cross Line, 173
Reed, Henry, 16
Returned Californian, The, 20-21
Rice, Luther, 97
Richards, Belle Luther, 80
Ringleader, Ship, 110, 152
Roberts, John, 128
Ropes, Joseph, 35
Rockwell, John, 128
Rocky at The Dockside, 74, 75
Rodgers, Williams C., 12
Rollin' King, xx, xxi
Rosamond Sloop HMS, 140
Ruben Ranzo, 172-173
Russell, E., 133
Rutstien, Captain Michael, 128
Ryan, Gerry, 86
Ryan's Mammoth Collection, 16

- S -

Sail, Power and Steam Museum, 124
Sailor's Early Home, The, 37-39
Sailor's Farewell, 54
Sailor's Magazine and Naval Journal, 49
Sailor's Watch At Sea, The, 61

Salem and California Mining and Trading Expedition, 7
Salem Cadet Band, 20
Salem Evening News, 107
Salem Gazette, 9, 44, 60 61, 62, 63, 65, 66, 68, 72, 74, 77, 90, 92 102, 118, 120, 132, 136, 138
Salem Glee Club, 103
Salem Mercury, 70
Salem Music Co., 104
Salem Public Library, 12-15
Salem's Bright Valley, 80
Salem Vessels and Their Voyages, 140
Sally Brown, 165, 172
San Francisco Company, xvii
Santa Anna, 168
Saunders, Charles, 141
Scott, Sir Walter, 52
Sea Mew, Bark, 75
Sea Ran High, The, 49
Seaman's Distress, 24
Seaman's Home, The, 77
Seaman's Orphan and Children's Friend Society, 107
Seaman, The, 60-61
Seamen's Bethel, 107
Servant of Rosemary Lane, 184
Shannon, Brig, 150-151
Shanties From the Seven Seas, xxii
Sharp, Cecil, 50
Sharply Its Breath the Vessel Feels, 51
Shay, Frank, 2

Shenandoah, 174
Ship Bengal at Sea, 44
Ships and Sailors of Old Salem, 29-31
Ship's Cabin The Most Unusual Room in New England, 158-159
Ship's Carpenter, 29-31
Silber, Irwin, 5
Silsbee, George Z., 52, 123
Silsbee, Nathaniel, xxii, 53, 54
Silsbee, William Zachariah, 141
Silver, William, 45, 46
Smith, William, 75
Smyth, Mary Winslow, 202, 206
Songs, Odes, and Other Poems, on Nautical Subjects, 62
Songs of the Great American West, 5
Songs of the People, xix
Songs of the Sailor and Lumberman, xxiii
Songs of the Sea and Sailors' Chanteys, 10-11
Songs of the Sea and Shore, xix
Songs of the Tall Ships, 46
Songs the Whalemen Sang, xix, 29-31, 46, 49
South Australia, xx, xxi
St. Paul, Ship, 109
Starboard List, 46
Storm at Sea in a Schooner, 103-104
Stone, Richard F., 141
Stormy Winds Do Blow, The, 24
Stowe, Phineas, 94-99

Sumatra, 74, 75, 123, 145
Sweet, Ralph, 16
Sweet William and Gentle Jenny, 82-84

- T -

Taber, Harry Persons, 27
Tabernacle Church, 94, 97, 106
Tale of the Sea, The, 104-105
Taria Topan, Barque, 156-187
Terror, 152
Th' Embargo, 120-121
The Stowaway Mouse, 74, 75
Thompson, Edward, 54
Today and Yesteryear, 86
Tom Pepper, 160-163
Traditional Ballad Index, 152
Trumbull, Captain Edward B., xxv, 156-187
Tuttle, Henry A., 5, 37

- U -

Union Fifth Reader, 37
Unknown Title, 117

- V -

Valpey, Jr., Joseph, 39, 41, 42, 84
Vaughan, Ship, 29-31
Vaughan Williams Memorial Library, 156-187
Vocal Library a collection of English, Scottish and Irish Songs, 77

Index

- W -

Waite and Pierce, 140
Walser, Bob, 160
Wandering Sailor, The, 53
Washington, General George, 133
Weatherly, F.E., 104
Webb, Annie Bertram, 156
Whale Catcher, 46
Whaling And Sailing Songs, From the Days of Moby Dick, 24
When Johnny Comes Marching Home Again, 20
While I'm at the Wheel, xxii
Whisky Johnny, 182-183
White, Eugene Richard, 27-28
Wide Missouri, The, 174-175
Wife Wrapped in Wether's Skin, 82
Williams, Alice, 94
Witch of the Wave, 2, 12-15
Witch of the Wave (tune), 16
Witchcraft, The, 12
Wood's Minstrel, 180
Worcester, Rev., 97
Written at Sea in a Heavy Gale, 70-71

- Y -

Yankee Jack, 102
Ye Golden Lamps of Heaven! Farewell, 124-125

Ye Mariners All, 128
Young, Larry, 128

- Z -

Zanzibar, 14, 117, 170
Zanzibar Work Song, 164-166

www.ingramcontent.com/pod-product-compliance
Lightning Source LLC
Chambersburg PA
CBHW051423290426
44109CB00016B/1412